This Isn't
The Movies

Parafine Press First Edition 2020
ISBN: 978-1-950843-09-1

Parafine Press
3143 West 33rd Street, Cleveland, Ohio 44109
www.parafinepress.com

Book and cover design by David Wilson

This Isn't
The Movies
25 Years in the Classroom

Charles Ellenbogen

Parafine Press
Cleveland Ohio

for Kirsten

FOREWORD

When I came back to Cleveland Schools for the second time as a principal, I had only one question for the CEO (that's what superintendents are called in districts taken over by mayoral control): "Can I hire my own faculty and staff?" I asked the same question over and over. I had no other questions. "Can I hire the teachers?"—Yes. "Can I hire the secretary?"—Yes. "Can I hire the security guards?"—No, but you can have input. "Fine."

I went through the list of every position I would need to start a "new and innovative" high school for kids who absolutely needed and deserved a school that could help them "envision, engage and excel," as our tagline would promise. I'm a big fan of Jim Collins' *Good to Great: Why Some Companies Make the Leap...and Others Don't,* and from my past experiences as a principal in both public and private schools, I know that the most important driver of success for any organization is to have the right people on the bus, in the right seats, and in complete agreement on the direction we are heading. In schools, the kids are fine; it's the adults you need to get right.

To that end, I was looking for two general groups of people: young, early career teachers and staff I could mentor and "mold in my evil image" and seasoned, midcareer teachers and staff like myself who were fed up with the system and seeking the freedom to try something new. As you will read, Charles's career has taken him around this country and the world. He's been a part of countless curricular initiatives, school structures, and demographics. He was searching as desperately as I was for something that actually works for kids in schools. I knew within minutes of meeting him that I not only needed him on the bus, but that I needed him in one of the front seats to help me navigate and tell me when I was veering off course. Charles is an introvert who is not afraid to share his thoughts. He will tell you if he thinks you are drifting, and I needed that kind of honesty if we were really going to do something different for our kids. We didn't always agree but we always knew the other was trying to make every decision in the best interests of our students. I have little patience for educators (and districts) who can't seem to grasp this concept and neither does Charles. Had I been able to keep hiring folks like Charles (I didn't think to ask, "Can I hire my own staff for more than just the first year?") maybe we would both still be at Eagle Academy, but that's for another book.

The late Rita Pierson says in her often viewed TED Talk *Every Kid Needs a Champion* that "kids don't learn from teachers they don't like" (2013). I would take her assertion further to suggest that kids don't learn from teachers they know don't care about them. The kids at Eagle Academy never questioned whether Mr. E cared about them. Charles did the things that most teachers that care about kids do: he called home, he went looking for you if you skipped class, he gently asked what was wrong if you were out of sorts, he celebrated your successes and told you he thought you could do even more when you thought it was good enough. But what sets Charles apart is his ability to marry his love for kids with his love for his subject area. Ask a high school teacher what they teach and they will often tell you their subject area— "I teach math." Ask an elementary school teacher and they will say, "I teach second graders." From what I observed, Charles puts them together and places the child before the subject to say, "I teach kids to love literature." Kids love him because he loves them. Kids love to read because he loves to read. Caring can be just that simple: love others and share what you love with them.

Now before you think Charles is some "touchy-feely" guy, you need to know that if you ask him if he would rather talk to you or read a book (he is never without at least one) he is going to pick the book every time. I loved coming through the empty cafeteria that was in the center of our school to find Charles sitting at one of the high-top tables reading during his planning period. Kids would come by and ask, "Hey Mr. E, what are you reading?" He'd glance up, tell them about the book, and usually finish with, "I'll get you a copy if you want to read it too." Again, another simple concept:model that reading is a fun and enjoyable use of time. In our second year, we took a small group of students to present with us (on the police/community relations unit described later) at a conference in San Antonio. As we waited to board our flight, Charles looked up from his book to see all four students scrolling through their phones. He got up and came back with four books from the airport bookstore he thought each might enjoy. He handed them out and said, "At the airport, we read while waiting for the flight." Most of us spend our time talking about the importance of reading; Charles does whatever it takes (or costs) to make it happen.

As Charles got to know each student better, he became a

genuine book whisperer. He simply couldn't accept that there was not at least one genre, style, or author a kid couldn't get excited about. It's entirely possible Charles just talks to kids (and adults too, for that matter) for the sole purpose of helping them find their next book. And then we all found our next books together because everyone was talking about Mike Brown and Tamir Rice. And Charles proved that when you focus on the needs of kids, even after twenty-five years of teaching, and being pretty great at what you do, you can become an even better teacher.

Gloria Ladson-Billings's concept of culturally responsive pedagogies and practices as described in *The Dreamkeepers: Successful Teachers of African-American Children* is the framework I use for my research and personal efforts to get better as a teacher and leader (1994). Ladson-Billings says that students need to be able to see themselves in the curriculum and teachers need to make space for this to happen. In practice, it is rare to see it done well (Schauer, 2018). It almost always gets hijacked to a place where the teacher (usually white and female) ends up telling the kids what they are seeing, how it should relate to them, and coming up with some test to make sure they saw it her way. The beauty of the Eagle Academy unit on police/community relations that became the yearlong seminar was that Charles saw his role as resource finder and listener. His voice was never louder than the kids. His experiences didn't frame the conversation. He followed their lead. He got them the books they asked for, the speakers they wanted to hear (including Tamir Rice's aunt, Tonya Goldbsy) and got out of the way. When the planned time for the unit was over, he just kept it going, because the kids were driving the learning by then and isn't that what we should want and encourage our high school kids to do? Did they miss opportunities to read genres and authors he originally planned for the year? Of course. But when you really get serious about putting the needs of kids first, you understand that life doesn't come in weekly units and complex topics are better addressed with extended study, research presentations, and poetry slams than surveys of literature and publisher-made multiple choice tests. Charles knew all this, but the kids at Eagle Academy and their seminar on police/community relations made it real and viable. The kids made Charles an even better teacher and I was blessed to witness this growth as his principal and colleague.

The journey Charles lays out in the pages that follow is full of stories from his experiences in a diverse collection of schools and contexts. The constant that weaves them together is that, in all of them, Charles is Charles. He doesn't compromise or waver from loving kids, his subject, or demanding that decisions be made in the best interests of children. This brings him accolades as much as it gets him into trouble, but it is the educational hill he has dedicated a career to climb and I am honored to have met him along the way. I invite you to join him as you read his story and reflect on your own journey.

Margaret (Peggy) Schauer, Ph.D.

Former principal of Eagle Academy, Cleveland Metropolitan School District
Current Assistant Professor of Secondary Education, John Carroll University

References

Collins, J. C. (2001). *Good to Great: Why Some Companies Make the Leap ... and Others Don't.* New York, NY: HarperBusiness.

Ladson-Billings, G. (2009). *The Dreamkeepers: Successful Teachers of African American Children* (2nd ed.). San Francisco, Calif.: Jossey-Bass Publishers.

Schauer, M. (2018). "Vygotsky for the Hood": Connecting teacher prior life experiences and university teacher preparation curriculums for service in urban schools. Teaching and Teacher Education, 74, 1-9.

TED Talk (2013). *Rita Pierson: Every Kid Needs a Champion.* [video] Available at: http://www.ted.com/talks/rita_pierson_every_kid_needs_a_champion/transcript?language=en.

A Note on Names

When I started to sketch out ideas for this book, I got some feedback about my decision to use the names of people, even the names of schools. People felt attacked. Kirsten, my wife, worried about legal issues. So you will find very few names in these pages. I thought about pseudonyms, but didn't want to get bogged down by the need to keep track of them. I worried about style, the awkwardness involved with naming people without using their names. I've never cared for the pronoun "one" that I foolishly taught to my students for many years. I haven't disguised people, so readers who know some of the stories will recognize the characters.[1] And if some sentences are clumsy as a consequence, forgive me. You will see, as you read, that a desire *not* to make people feel attacked is a kind of growth for me.

---

1 Anna Burns recently won the Booker Prize for Milkman, in which she does not use names. So, you know, I'm trendy.

Introduction

Some years ago, I don't remember exactly when or why, I made myself a promise. If I stayed in teaching for twenty-five years, I told myself, I would try to write a book.

I am not sure what I anticipated would be so magical about twenty-five years. I certainly didn't expect to be preparing for my first year at my tenth school. And I don't think the fact that I've taught for twenty-five years makes me wiser or better or more deserving of a higher salary than teachers who have taught for fewer years. I have certainly fulfilled Malcolm Gladwell's 10,000 hours[2] and, given my somewhat unique path, I think I have some things that are worth saying—to teachers (especially newer ones), to administrators, to consultants, to policy makers, and to the general public. While I am just *one* teacher, I do think I have a voice, a story that is seldom told.

When I visit the education shelves at bookstores and libraries,[3] I often find books by and about education experts that claim to have solutions or a true grasp of things, or I find instruction manuals, ranging from how to prepare for an alphabet soup of tests to how to teach writing or how to teach with poverty in mind. Though I know they are out there, and I'll recommend some along the way, I do not find many

---

2 I just came back from a conference that questioned the validity of his theory.

3 Okay, more often bookstores.

books about the current lived experiences of teachers written while they are teaching. The chapters that follow chronicle my experiences at ten different schools in seven different cities that shaped who I am as a teacher. With Chimamanda Adichie's warning about "the danger of a single story"[4] in mind, I want to share my reality, my narrative, my lived experience as I'm living it. In that spirit, I'll interrupt myself in between chapters to offer what I will call rants about the day-to-day headaches of being a teacher.

I am no hero. There will be no movie about me. You will not find Robin Williams here. Or Edward James Olmos. Not even Jack Black. But I can say with confidence that my experiences are shared with countless teachers around the country. If you want an unvarnished look at an often thankless yet incredibly rewarding job, or you want to commiserate with a fellow educator, then this book is for you. I hope you'll annotate this and argue with me in the margins. Most importantly, I hope you'll teach. Stick with it. I can't say it'll get easier, but it'll never stop bringing you joy.

---

4 If you haven't watched it, please do (https://www.ted.com/talks/chimamanda_adichie_the_danger_of_a_single_story). Go ahead; I'll wait.

1
Georgetown Day School
Washington, D.C.

Every teacher is shaped by their own experiences as a student. So before jumping into my twenty-five year career, it's worth starting with what I learned on the other side of the classroom. I went to Chevy Chase Elementary School in suburban Maryland for first grade. We had "open classrooms," areas partitioned by rolling chalkboards, and show and tell. I don't remember much else. I later encountered a description of this school as a case study of school desegregation, but I can't speak to that at all other than to say that my mother did not want any of us to be part of that particular social experiment.

That summer, my parents divorced, and the decision was made to send my siblings and me to private school. They took us around to different schools and let us discover the place that fit us best. I picked Georgetown Day,[5] where I was fortunate to have a tall, patient, New Zealand woman named Robyn[6] as my second-grade teacher.

Fifth grade was my first disaster. I got suspended for throwing a pair of scissors at another student when he said something about my mother. But fifth grade was redeemed by

---

5 I am still amazed that my mother let us (my brother, sister, and I) all go to different private schools. How did we ever get everywhere we needed to be? Kirsten (my wife) and I have two children. The logistics are intimidating.

6 We called our teachers by their first names. Like so much of my school experience, this had a powerful impact on me.

sixth because sixth grade is when I met Clay.

Clay, slim, mustached, prematurely grey, would end up playing a big role in my life. But it was his teaching partner, Norinne, who gave me my first epiphany about teachers. She was late one day and told us the story of why, about starting out for school, finding she'd forgotten something, and returning home to have her family laugh at her forgetfulness and then driving to school. Something shifted in my understanding of the world. *My teacher had a family.* I was under the spell of *Knight Rider* at the time, and I think I imagined that teachers went into the back of a truck when they weren't teachers. But not Norinne; she had a family. She was a *person*.

Clay was an oddball. He told shaggy dog jokes, read us O. Henry stories, and played Muddy Waters 45s. Like all sixth graders, we learned about ancient civilizations[7], but what I remember is that Clay made an effort to understand my emotional volatility. Instead of storming out of class, I learned, because of his coaching, to ask permission to take walks to calm myself down. I think he struggled with his own temper. Perhaps I was drawn to him because he was the first adult I'd met who made no attempt to hide his disdain for adults who were foolish. He took me—all of us—seriously.

Georgetown Day was a unique place, a leftover from the 60s perhaps. Teachers would show pictures of themselves sitting in trees to conduct class. The high school was in two adjacent converted office buildings. Students lounged and studied in hallways. We left our lockers unlocked. We did not

---

7 I think our daughter came home last year with an assignment I had in sixth grade. I admit I haven't worked my knowledge of Mesopotamia into my daily life.

have chairs in our common area, so we sat on the floor during town meetings about topics like whether it was fair that boys got to take their shirts off on the adjacent patio but girls didn't.

One year, Allen Ginsberg did a reading at a school assembly. The English teachers were in a tizzy for days before his visit, so I got there early to sit in one of the front rows. My reaction to Ginsberg is memorialized in a photo taken that day. I sit there, shaggy-haired, in one of the first few rows, my hands on either side of my cheeks (think Macaulay Culkin in the poster for *Home Alone*). I remember thinking, "Why in the world is this guy saying those words and spitting at me? And what is that instrument he's playing?"

The school was not for everyone. Like any D.C. private school, a lot of the students were from powerful and influential families. I was classmates with the son of a congressman from Kansas who later became the secretary of agriculture. That classmate now makes movies in Hollywood. I enjoyed a comment during one of the recent presidential election years that presidents may send their children to Sidwell (where my brother went and, later, the Obama children), but you could hold cabinet meetings in the carpool lane at Georgetown Day. I ran into a baseball teammate years later, and he told me that he'd found our school to be very stressful. I'm not sure why he thought it was important for me to know this after so many years. I suspect a lot of my other classmates felt the same way, though.

In the entrance to the K-8 building[8], there is a sculpture of a grasshopper. This became our school mascot.

---

8 I know it seems like I'm going backwards; bear with me.

Periodically, debates would emerge about it that would have us considering something more aggressive instead, like the Generals. But we never made any progress. One of our biggest rivalries was with the school in Langley, home of the CIA. Their nickname may have been the only one less intimidating than ours: the Swallows.[9]

***

A colleague of mine once offered a theory that teachers tend to want to teach a grade level that was, for some reason, important to them, either positively or negatively. Some part of us, she speculated, had gotten stuck in that year or range of years. There has to be some reason teachers select the grade ranges they do. When asked what they want to teach, teachers will invariably say, for example, "I won't teach anything above fifth grade." I'm the same way. For a while, I never wanted to go below seventh grade.[10] Now it's ninth. I never imagined going above twelfth. I recently tested the waters by teaching one college class a year; the jury's still out.

In any event, the years that shaped me most, for better *and* for worse, were high school. And one of the most central

---

9 After being a grasshopper, I went on to become a Maroon in college. (Big rivalry: the Violets.) As a teacher, I've been a Hurricane, a Bear, a Knight, an Eagle, a Knight (again), a Knight (yes, again), a Bear (second time), a Red Raider (wince), and an Eagle (second time). I'm told the principal of my new school plans to allow our students to select the mascot.

10 As an April Fool's joke, I once switched places with the first-grade teacher for a morning. Longest. Morning. Of. My. Life. It was over twenty years ago; I still haven't recovered.

Charles Ellenbogen   21

experiences of my high school career was my participation in the school's theater program.

Somewhere in this social media world, there is a page dedicated to those, like me, who absolutely loved our high school theater program. Now that I have children of my own, one of whom is particularly interested in theater, I have only gained more appreciation for my own experience. I have long wondered what made it work. On the surface, the success of the program is obvious. The program can boast of actors and writers on Broadway, on TV, movie makers, etc. (Me? I go to plays. And try to bring students. And I recently helped stage a student production of that immortal classic, *The Cosmic Fruit Bowl*.)

But I think its success runs deeper than that. While the program was largely in the hands of one person, Laura, I don't think it was a case of cult of personality. And it wasn't just a case of "the theater crowd," though some of my classmates have memories of cliquishness. In contrast, several former classmates have described the theater program as being particularly welcoming, even necessary for the LGBT students, something of which I was oblivious.

Whatever it was that made us so close, I have to give Laura credit for at least two things. She had incredibly high standards—for herself and for all of us. I loved the way she rejected the idea that there was anything she—and therefore, we—could not do, even with a limited budget (and the fact that we produced our shows in the gym). Her spirit was contagious, and the colleagues that worked with her radiated that spirit as well. She gave students a lot of responsibility. A LOT. And you had to earn it, especially on the technical side. You started on a crew and worked your way up. A guild system, I have since been told. And it was not all about talent. I was not particularly skilled at designing and building sets, for example, but I'd earned my chance to design and build a set for *Pygmalion* that was, or at least was supposed to be, in the round. It ended up being more like three-quarters.

I think the element that has most carried over into my own teaching is the way Clay and Laura treated us like adults. I don't know whether it was deliberate; it just was. Laura let us fail before that became fashionable. She had to. She couldn't do everything herself. We had two intense arguments. In the first case, she could have pulled rank when I challenged her. I know a lot of teachers who would have made my comments into a discipline issue, but she didn't. She took me seriously, even preventing her class from entering the room until we'd resolved our disagreement. That was how she did things. Instead of leaning on her authority, she inspired us to work hard to live up to her expectations. I've had numerous students tell me that this was what they appreciated about their experience in my class. For this, I thank Laura.

The second argument that I had with Laura is still a source of regret. In my senior year, the school was preparing to move into a new building that was designed for us and would provide more space for extracurriculars. Mine was the last class that would graduate from the old one, and as someone who participated in a lot of extracurriculars I was asked to speak at the groundbreaking. From time to time, I consulted with Laura about drafts of my speech. She was very supportive, but on the day of the ceremony she objected to two specific paragraphs in my final draft. The first was about how there would be no black male students graduating with me. The second was about how teachers were leaving, and that the school had very few black male teachers. I thought those facts were disappointing in light of our history as one of the first integrated schools, and worthy of highlighting to the assembled masses.

Laura's response was unequivocal. She said that if I included those two paragraphs, she would unplug the microphone while I was speaking. I told my mother of my dilemma, and she simply told me, "I love you no matter what you decide to do." I left the paragraphs out.

For a long time, I counted that decision as one of my biggest regrets in life, but I think I was kidding myself. I should have been forthright from the start. Who knows what would have happened? In four years, Laura had given me every reason in the world to trust her. And then I hadn't honored that. Would she have helped me mold my concerns into something appropriate? Would she have convinced me that the occasion was not appropriate? Would I have withdrawn from the ceremony because I wasn't allowed to speak my mind? I don't know, but I should have found out.[11]

Rant: That Class

If you haven't had it yet, you will. That class. Some demonic force in the universe contrives to put the worst combination of students together in your room

---

11 As much as I cherish the place, I do wonder what gets lost when all of the money comes rolling in. I see what some of my classmates are able to donate,and I think that I don't belong there anymore. For the first time, I actually thought about attending a reunion (the thirtieth), but I felt all of my awkwardness—both past and present—come swimming back in. I didn't go.

one period each day, and it all just goes very, very
badly.

For me, this year, it's sixth period. And I know
better, by now, to label them that way. A kind of
perverse pride can emerge among the students and
confirmation bias can get its icy talons into the teacher.
So each day, I try to be optimistic. Today, I tell myself,
will be the day. I am always sure that all of that energy,
if turned in the right direction, can produce greatness.

Today was not that day.

As always, there are a handful of students who
look from you to their peers and back again with the
weariness and wariness of fourteen year olds who
have been through this before. They are experienced
enough not to blame the teacher. They sit up close,
but not so close that they might actually grab a tiny
piece of learning that finds its way through the noise.
And that's what it was today: noise.

I mean, I've had bad incidents, even fights, happen
in my classroom. I've had particularly problematic students. I've had outbursts and swearing and, like zillions
of others of teachers, I've battled music and phones for
students' attention. And there's some of that this year,
but mostly, it's noise. Slow, steady noise. This constant
chatter that sends a clear message: "We're here, and
we're not going to do anything big enough to get us in
serious trouble. We're going to do just enough to irritate
you and then laugh at your temper and frustration."

I just don't have the energy for the yelling
anymore—not that it was ever very productive. And

I want students to be in the class. They seem to care little about being the only section not to manage to have anyone ready for their final presentations. The days just go on. We were asked for more referrals at a meeting this week, so I wrote a few this afternoon and then, as I always do, I felt badly. What good will they do the student who pulled her chair closer to the wall so her phone could charge as she quietly had a conversation? Or the young man who, despite my repeated requests, drifted to the back of the classroom and was unsurprisingly sucked down the rabbit hole of his phone and his friend (and her phone)? The first quarter is almost over. Will grades get their attention? Will parents? One parent even came and sat in class with her daughter. That helped— for a while.

Am I too nice, as some students claim? Students who had me in the past would chuckle at the accusation. Should I do a seating chart? Teach differently? I have tried both and have learned what they teach you in the parenting books: Don't administer any punishment that you don't want to endure.

Tomorrow, I am thinking that I will seat those who showed some interest in class today in the inner circle, and I will just work with them. Some from the outside may get intrigued enough to quiet down and join in. I don't know. I'll probably change my mind a million times between now and tomorrow afternoon. I know the goal is to engage every child, but right now, I just can't do it.

2
The University of Chicago
Chicago, IL

My older brother attended the University of Chicago, and I visited him there a few times. He wanted me to like the place, so he found a class for me to audit. The students were reading a Greek play, and I loved it. I think I even participated. I was hooked.

I didn't know at the time that the university's reputation was as conservative as Georgetown Day's was liberal. I know now that the juxtaposition of the liberal Georgetown Day and the conservative University of Chicago made for odd bedfellows. Georgetown Day was usually a pipeline to Oberlin, for example. Still, Chicago, like Georgetown Day before it, worked for me.

My answers to the housing questionnaire led me a dorm on the edge of campus, Breckinridge. Despite thinking of myself as a rather conventional sort of a person, I kept finding myself at the edges of things. I was sent my roommate's address and was startled to learn that he was from Colombia. I'm not sure who wrote first, but he definitely wrote the better and funnier letter, mocking all sorts of Colombian stereotypes (drug dealer, coffee farmer, etc.) and assuring me that he didn't fit into any of those categories. And it was in that dorm where I met Kirsten, my wife of more than twenty-five years.

Chicago had a core curriculum, which was probably good because I had no idea what to study. I entered college with the intention of majoring in political science or something in that family. I grew up, as you may recall in D.C. Perhaps that's all I knew? But someone, maybe one of my brother's friends, introduced me to the New Collegiate Division and the major called Fundamentals: Issues and Texts.[12] This required an application and deciding to center on what we called a burning question. The apocryphal example was the student whose question was, "Is there such a thing as a just war?" After graduation, the story went, he joined the military to find out. I can't remember what question I used for my application, but I was admitted. This meant I was required to register[13] for the introductory sequence of courses the next year. It was in the first quarter[14] of that sequence that I met the professor who would have a deep impact on me, and not just because he became my advisor.

Mr. Kass was a gentle and probing guide. I loved going to his office hours. My classmates and I joked about the genius emanating from his office because, you see, he was an MD and a PhD, which made him the smartest person any of us knew. He gave me one of the most memorable pieces of

---

12 As all Fundamentals majors know, including the one I married, this major had to be accompanied by an explanation whenever our transcripts were sent out. But no one misunderstood it more than the parents of a college girlfriend who heard me say, "Fundamentalism."

13 I went to the University of Chicago when we boasted as being ranked the #300 on the list of 300 top party schools. One of our big social occasions was the tradition of sleeping out on the quads to secure a high number for registration. One year, as I wound my way through the halls to register, a newspaper reporter asked me why I'd slept out for a high number. I was so exhausted, I couldn't come up with a response. Maybe I never had one.

14 Chicago operated (operates?) on a quarter system. It was. . . intense.

feedback on an essay I've ever received. He wrote, "Your first two pages are as good as any I read; unfortunately, you wrote six pages." He could get away with that. Like Laura, he made us want to rise the occasion. Once he suggested I read a few pages of his book *Toward a More Natural Science*; I read the whole thing and went to see him at office hours to talk about it. He was stunned that I'd read the whole thing. Later, when I registered for a class with him in which I was pretty far out of my league, he came across me working on the top floor of the library—papers, books, notes, index cards, etc.—spread across a library table generally meant for at least two people. He asked about the project. I told him it was the five-page paper for his class. He raised his eyebrows, which was a gold star among his acolytes. I got an A-. (I came across that paper a few years ago. I have no idea what I was talking about.)[15]

Mr. Kass and his wife, Amy, were both a huge influence on me, on a lot of us. They invited us to their homes for dinners. We were like family. I wanted to be around them as much as possible, so I enrolled in a class that both of them were teaching on *War and Peace*. The class started at roughly the same time that the first Gulf War began. I remember this because someone knocked on the door during one class and asked if anyone wanted to join an anti-war protest on the quad at that moment. No one moved and Mr. Kass dismissed the intruder with a few words.

That class was also powerful to me for another reason. My father had been to Russia several times for work. With his

---

15 As for the Nietzche paper my father kept in the same box, it was like I was writing in another language.

encouragement, I went on a high school trip there. So, before the class started, I invited him to read along with me. We would talk about our progress once a week. I can't remember the names of the characters[16] involved, but at one point, a young man wants to get married and goes to ask his father's permission. His father tells him to wait a year. The young man waits the year, gets married, and never visits his father again. I was pretty much in the same place in life. Kirsten and I took a bus to D.C. in part to attend an anti-war protest and in part for me to talk to my father about our engagement. He, too, asked me to wait. I was not as obedient a son as the Russian one; we weren't going to wait. He and I didn't talk much about marriage after that.

After the Kass's class on *War and Peace*, I would cut across the Midway to a class called "Crime and Punishment" that did not, in fact, center on the Dostoyevsky[17] novel. It did include a careful look at *Antigone*, a play I'd also read in Greek that would become the center of the final version of my Fundamentals question. Once upon a time, I had my Fundamentals question memorized. We all did. For now, you'll have to settle for my best effort to reconstruct it: How does a person react when he[18] is faced with loyalties to two places that conflict with each other? Antigone believes she has a responsibility to her family, to her sense of the Gods to bury her brother who turned "traitor." Creon, the representative of the state, forbids it, but she does it anyway.

---

16 Insert your own joke about Russian character names here.

17 Unlike Nietzsche, I did spell this one right on the first try.

18 Despite focusing on a female protagonist, I'm sure I just wrote "he." This was 1991.

Besides being an intellectual mentor, Mrs. Kass would be the first to help me make a connection with a Chicago public school. Unfortunately, it was on the far north side of the city. (The university is on the south side of Chicago.[19]) She was also the first to ask me about my determination to work at a public school. I don't know what my answer was, but I do remember thinking it was feeble. I knew I wanted to be at a public school. Maybe I'd seen too many teacher movies. I knew I had to come up with a better reason, not for Mrs. Kass, but for myself.

At this first public school, Sullivan High School, I mostly observed. One teacher allowed me a day on "Sir Gawain," which a student tried to derail with his comments about the war with Iraq. I helped with a unit on *Anthem*.[20] One of my most prominent memories, though, is of the fights in the hallway, in particular the inevitable crowd and the viciousness with which girls would fight each other. That hadn't been my experience at Georgetown Day. As I set off to make a career in teaching, though, I'd find out there was a lot more about Georgetown Day and Chicago that wasn't anything like the rest of the world.

Rant: Certification

I am not against certification. Doctors have to be certified, electricians have to be certified, food

---

19 I'll give you a moment here to sing the Jim Croce song, "Bad, Bad Leroy Brown." If you don't know it, look it up.

20 This was long before I had any real idea who Ayn Rand was. I taught the book again in the spring of my twenty-fourth year. The Ayn Rand Institute sends them to you for free.

service workers have to be certified, and so on. It's only natural and right that teachers should be certified as well. But it's interesting that we require this for PK-12 teachers and not college professors. To teach in college, you need to do ... what? Publish something? Have a certain degree? Either one presumably means that you know a lot about your subject, though it's not a guarantee. But does it mean you know how to teach? No, not likely. You will almost certainly do what a lot of teachers of any level do—you will teach how you were taught.

Does certification mean you are a good teacher? No. It *should* mean you have a core base of knowledge that your program has decided is necessary for a teacher. There should, for example, be something to help prospective teachers understand the age group they'll be teaching. We have too many teacher certification programs, so there's no real quality control. It's too easy to be accepted, both because the schools need the money and because we need so many teachers. This is, in part, why the pay stays so low. Every single message we get from everyone everywhere is that we're replaceable.

So should we do as Finland has done? Make it harder to be admitted and raise the pay? I think it's worth trying. Before you jump down my throat and say we're not like Finland, I am not suggesting that we try it everywhere all at once, i.e., the American Way. Nor am I suggesting that we continue our habits of experimenting on poor people of color. But there is, somewhere, an appropriate place for a pilot program. What about private schools, which sometimes don't require certification? There are plenty of great teachers in private schools—some who are certified, some with advanced degrees. And luckily (though not coincidentally), there are often funds for good professional development. Teachers who keep learning and who maintain their humility are the ones who will improve. If you stay still, if you become complacent and stagnate, increasingly, you will blame things on students, the changes going on around you, administrators, etc. Anyone but yourself.

Then there's the issue of those of us who move from state to state. To get certified in a new state, you often have to take a test—no matter how long you've been teaching. This strikes me as ridiculous. I believed, for a time, in the National Board Certification process. But the group—the National Board for Professional Teaching Standards—hasn't been able to maintain its initial momentum and get the support of all of the states. The certificate can get you some supplementary funds, but I've always had to fight for them. Ultimately, when my certificate expired, I decided not to try to renew it. Apparently, getting one day older made me lose as much knowledge and skill as crossing a state line.

At the time of this writing, I am attempting to renew my license in Ohio. There are two things, insofar as I understand it, that stand between me and not having to deal with all of this crap for another five years:

1) WebCheck—I have to have my fingerprints taken to make sure I haven't gotten into any trouble in the last five years.

2) Technical Upgrade—I submitted all of my hours and Continuing Education Units a few months ago. I was told recently that they haven't been evaluated and I haven't charged for converting hours to CEUs because there's some sort of district level computer upgrade happening. That didn't stop the state from taking $200 as an application fee.

My first IPDP (Individualized Professional Development Plan or, I kid you not, Ippy Dippy) was rejected, so I revised it and submitted a second draft. I have proof that I paid the $200. I have proof that my certificate has expired. Now, I just wait. And get my fingerprints taken.

This is how the state of Ohio wants me to spend my time.

In sum:

• Make certification meaningful and reward it accordingly.

• Reduce the bureaucracy involved in switching schools, states, subjects, roles.

• Require private schools to have some kind of continuing education requirement.

• Standardized tests are just as meaningless for

prospective teachers as they are for students.

• Stop treating teachers as a constant source of revenue.

• Relevant agencies need to work together to make this easier for teachers—why can't there be a database for my continuing education units? If you offer something, then you're given a code and a window of time, and you give the participants credit. Instead, I have to collect a piece of paper (sometimes I've paid for it) and submit copies to another agency. And so on. . .

3
The Harvard School
Chicago, IL

Graduation meant it was time to find a job, and I didn't really know how to do that. I applied to the private schools I knew about in Chicago. I got an interview at the Lab School, adjacent to the University of Chicago in Hyde Park. I sought Mr. Kass' advice, and he suggested a sample lesson involving pennies that I have since used often. But first, the interview. This was the first time I heard a question that I've come to loathe: 'Do you know how many resumes I've received for this position?"

In case any of you out there are in the position of hiring and use this question or have considered this question, here is what those of us sitting uncomfortably on the other side of the desk would like to say in response: "I don't care." Or: "Do you know how many resumes I've sent out?"[21]

I didn't get the job, though I'd later sub for the man who did. I was a terrible sub—at the Lab School and elsewhere. Not for lack of effort, though. I just had absolutely no sense of timing. I would finish lesson plans much too quickly and have to scramble to fill up the remaining time—with math games, mostly. Or sometimes, creative writing prompts.

In between subbing opportunities, I worked low-level

---

21 I later wrote a one-act about my interview experiences. It didn't go any further than my desk drawer, but it was cathartic.

theater jobs. The odd hours and low pay were challenging during our first year of marriage. There was a stretch in a bookstore, but given my addiction to books, I likely broke even there. (At best.)

The Lab School did yield a summer opportunity: a creative writing course. I missed a blatant case of plagiarism. I rankled one student because I found his stories about plane hijackings lacked credibility. "Write what you know," I repeated. That's what I was taught, so that's what I taught others. I now tell students to "write what you want to know." But that was the extent of my toolbox then.[22] I struggled to fill the class time.

Then, one of Kirsten's colleagues heard about a job opening at the Harvard School—a very old private school on 47th and Ellis, the very edge and very corner of my experience of Hyde Park-Kenwood. Think Elijah Mohammed, Louis Farrakhan. Later: the Obamas. If you look up the school, you will quickly learn two things. First, it is now closed. Second, it was central to the Leopold and Loeb murder case, a fact which we did not advertise in our brochures.

I do not remember much about this interview, but I do remember signing the contract and the principal telling me that the salary was not enough to start a family. I've never been shy about discussing salaries. I think the taboo against it is sometimes a tool used to intimidate people, and keep them from discovering whether they're being paid in an equitable manner. My salary for that first year in 1992 was $15,500. In any event, all I remember about my first day is the last period. A student, a senior, had his hand up for much of the period, but I was having none of it. It was, I told myself, my time to talk. So I kept talking and talking and talking. Finally, with maybe five or ten minutes left, I called on him. His question: "Can you tell us your name?"

***

The Harvard School was a good place for me to start, I think. My principal, after I'd had a particularly rough day, told me that what he liked about teaching is that you got to come back the next day and that, more often than not, the students had forgotten about whatever had made the day before feel so lousy for you. It's advice I've kept close at hand since then and have passed on to many others. I was allowed to make mistakes.

The Harvard School is tough to describe. We had a somewhat transient student population. We tended to get students who were getting lost in public schools and needed a kind of tune-up before they could return. Their parents were involved enough to recognize this need and resourceful enough to afford the kinds of small classes we offered. All of the students were black. A majority, if not a large majority of the teachers were white. Both principals I worked for there were white. Class sizes were small. In general, though, I really didn't know what I was doing, especially with those students who had special needs.

What I lacked in terms of training and strategies, I tried to make up for with energy. We read books that were challenging, and I tried to choose subjects that I thought would appeal to African American students. One student would eventually report being assigned similar titles in college and being grateful to me for the preparation. The librarian congratulated me on getting the students to read. Other students struggled. I did not have any idea how to help a student who couldn't spell the name of our school correctly. I tried to keep the students engaged. I went on a soapbox about how wrong Coca-Cola was for trying to introduce the word "phat" into their advertising. We debated ebonics. We discussed the teacher (not at our school) who'd picked up a long-rumored set of math problems based on drug transactions and actually used them in class. I had almost no ideas, except for yelling, about dealing with classroom behavior, or working with colleagues (much less getting along with some of them).

I remember my bubble of naivete bursting when I learned that two of our female students had children by the same father, so they'd been placed in separate grades to try to prevent conflict. There was also my first experience with a student who was being abused at home. Some of our students were involved with gangs and drugs. A student I had in eighth grade showed up driving a fancy car the next year. One senior plagiarized Camille Paglia for his final project and then set another student's hair on fire. I was far from the rarified halls of Georgetown Day. And my energy could not compensate for my lack of skills.

After that first year, we got a new principal. And we had budget problems, so the staffing situation changed quickly, and I ended up with a British Literature course I hadn't anticipated. I was still at a loss when it came to managing a grade book and was grateful that our motorcycle-riding math teacher was willing to guide me. We had a science teacher no one could figure out, and he ended up being asked to leave after the first quarter. Discipline issues persisted. Students came and went and sometimes came again.

I organized some field trips, mostly to see plays. One time we went to an art exhibit. Another time, a dance performance. I tried to help students get into college. (Some did; I'm not sure how many stayed.) Having learned enough to recognize some of the seeds of a gang conflict, I made a student turn his hat around when he was confronted by someone in the neighborhood as we walked to see *Othello* at a local theater. I took some students to hear Malcolm X's widow speak and mistakenly allowed some students to return in a private car. My exasperated principal explained the risks involved. They returned safely and with lunch from McDonalds. We went to see a morning matinee of *Of Mice and Men* and required the students to buy their lunch at a restaurant opened by the father of one of their classmates. I'd never had jerk chicken before. (It was good. I should check to see if his place is still open.)

That second year I volunteered to coach the basketball team. There was a parent who claimed that I, as the basketball coach, discriminated against her son because he was light skinned. I didn't know how to respond. I didn't want to say, "He's just not very good." But it was the first time I'd heard such a thing. Did people really discriminate against students of color because they were light skinned? I don't know how that ended. I taught the student how to set screens and how to run a pick and pop. He could make wide-open three-pointers. Sometimes.

I was in the middle of basketball practice when the principal asked if I would be on the Development Committee. I agreed in order to get rid of him. As a member of the Development Committee, I helped organize our annual fundraiser. The only reason it was successful the first year is that someone I invited was running a pyramid scheme, so he had a lot of cash to spend. One teacher threw a fit when she wasn't given a free ticket. I gave her one that one of my relatives, who lived too far away to attend and was just being supportive, had purchased. When I asked the chair what the money would be used for, he said, "You know those checks you all got today? Now they won't bounce."

This first year presented my initial encounter with English Teacher Syndrome.[23] Watch a science teacher introduce herself. The reaction will be reverent. "A science teacher—Ooh! Ah! They must be smart!" Math teachers get a similar response. Even history teachers get asked about which history class is their favorite or their specialty. English teachers, though, get one of two reactions:

1. "Uh-oh, I better watch my grammar!"[24]

2. An opinion offered about how to teach English.

You see, people who speak English, have taken an English class, and/or have a heartbeat think they are qualified to teach English. Science teachers are wizards touched by gods; English teachers are, as one later principal would put it, "a dime a dozen."

In this case, English Teacher Syndrome showed up at a faculty meeting.[25] We were all asked to do a curriculum review. The science team spoke as though from a pulpit. The math team all but received a standing ovation. I could barely get three words out before hearing feedback, suggestions, and criticisms. I was accused by one colleague of wanting primary students to write

---

23 I would call this ETS, but those initials are, unfortunately, taken.

24 If you are not sure, this is NOT funny.

25 The faculty meeting is the second dumbest invention ever; the platypus is the first.

essays about "the structure of a flower." It took all my strength not to reply, "I just want them to stop writing about the latest *Teenage Mutant Ninja Turtle* episode," though now I realize that that might have been all of the writing that particular teacher could elicit. When this frustrating meeting finally ended, I tried to relieve my stress by kicking a cabinet in the hallway. I forgot it was on wheels. It crashed into the glass case that held the fire extinguisher. The case broke, because of course it did.

The principal during my second year at the Harvard School brought in Bill Ayers to speak with us at a faculty meeting. This was, of course, long before he became known as Obama's "terrorist" friend.[26] I don't remember a great deal of what he said, but I was mesmerized. I believe I was the one who asked a question about classroom management. He said when he taught he only had two rules:

1. You *can* wear your hat.[27]
2. You can't interfere with someone else's learning.

I don't always have control over the rules about hats. But I still use the second rule.

During my first two years at the Harvard School, I learned a lot about teaching—and I learned that I loved it. I also learned that I didn't know enough to do it well. It was time, then, to go back to school.

---

26 Ayers, once a member of the Weather Underground, became a community organizer in Chicago and was in the education department at the University of Illinois at Chicago. Pictures of him with Obama became part of an effort to derail Obama's campaign momentum.

27 More about dress code and dress restrictions when I get to Cleveland.

Rant: Field Trips

I love field trips. Ask anyone who has ever worked with me. If I could, I'd have students out of the classroom almost every day. And I even have a stupidly persistent knack for being able to navigate the intense bureaucracy required to make them work. And I prepare for them not only using the materials the site offers me, but materials that I find and/or design myself. In sum, I feel like I'm doing my part.

So here's my challenge to places that are open to field trips, particularly museums. Do away with the docents. I know they are volunteers (and therefore cheap) and that many of them know a lot (though many have just memorized a lot). Many of them (in my experience) are older, which it makes it challenging for them to connect with high school students. And, in my experience, the large majority of them are white, which makes it challenging for them to connect with the students I've worked with for most of my life.

Obviously, it's easier (though not easy) to have students interact at the likes of a hands-on science museum. Students *do* stuff there.

My worst experience ever was at the Museum of Contemporary Art in Chicago. I saw an article about the work of Lorna Simpson. The focus was on her work on black women's hair and how it related to identity. I saw the exhibit myself first and took notes. The museum sent me slides. Somehow, I dug up a projector. I prepared an assignment for my students. I also prepared them for behavioral expectations. And the museum provided a free bus! (Field trip sites take note: Free and discounted tickets are great, but not if we can't get there. Include transportation when you write grants for funding.)

And then we got there. And we got a docent. And she had a plan, and she had no interest in mine. She was going to talk, and the students were going to listen. While the students found some of the other modern art pieces interesting, they did not have time to immerse themselves in the Simpson exhibit. Nor did they have the opportunity to form their own interpretations of any of the art; the docent simply told them what it "meant." She read from her notecards. I was fuming when we left.

Recently, I attended a field trip with my daughter because I'd seen the exhibit she was going to see and had sent students to see it with another teacher. It was a great photography exhibit featuring images and objects from the Civil Rights Movement. We got our docent, and he began to tell the students about the Movement. Now perhaps they needed it and perhaps they didn't, but they were there to look at the pictures—to learn how to "read" pictures and, in particular, these pictures. I'm a big fan of Visual Thinking Strategies.[28] You can practice in the classroom, and the process invariably elicits great

---

28 vtshome.org

observations, inferences, and insights. Let students be and let students do. Practice enough, and they will internalize the process. Have them write/draw and (gasp!) even talk right there in the gallery. Let them choose which images attract their attention. Let them make meaning—in small groups and / or individually—with the docent or teacher as the proverbial guide on the side. This means that an effective docent needs to "talk less."

So, teachers, do your part. Take these opportunities not as an opportunity to have someone else teach for a few hours, but as a spectacular chance to have everyone do some real learning. And museums, do away with the docent approach.

4
Wharton Arts Magnet Middle School
Nashville, TN

I went back to the University of Chicago for a Masters of Arts in Education, which would also qualify me for my teaching license. It was a one-year program (including the summer), and I was part of a cohort of students, maybe twelve or so, taught by the influential George Hillocks. I learned to appreciate him more after I finished the program, especially his books, but he was near the end of his run when I enrolled. He was clearly tired, and it showed.

Still, I learned a great deal in his classes, particularly about the teaching of writing. I had a chance to develop lessons and units that were the foundation of my first few years of teaching. I was recently reminded of the educational psychology course that I took as part of this program. I did poorly on a paper because I had used more than one thinker to analyze a student I was working with during my student-teaching experience. Apparently, I was supposed to have guessed that I could only use one thinker because I had to become part of someone's "school" of thinking. Philosophy of Education with Phil Jackson[29] was great, but should not have been in the spring. By then, our thoughts had turned to more practical things, like finding a job.

The English classes I had to choose from were absurd. I took a class that was, according to the professor, something

---

29 No relation to the basketball coach

he wanted to call "Airport Novels through the Ages." My aggravation about this class was compounded when I learned one of the great professors at the college, Wayne Booth, was teaching a summer class on high school classics, but it was only open to people who were already teaching.

There were other requirements that were equally ridiculous. I had to go to a professor and ask him to write a short paragraph explaining that a class I'd taken with him on Abraham Lincoln was actually an American history course. Lucky for me, he had a sense of humor. For some reason, I also had to take a test on Illinois history. I took it with a colleague in the cohort who was actually from Illinois, and I cheated. I think he knew, but didn't care. Shortly after that— before our year was over—the requirement was eliminated.

Hillocks had relationships with three main schools for the purpose of placing student teachers. Kirsten and I were car-less, and there was a perfectly good Chicago public school within walking distance of our apartment called Kenwood Academy. I accumulated some of my observation hours there and formed enough of a relationship with the department that two teachers agreed to co-mentor my student teacher efforts.

The two could not have been more different. The first, Jon Nemeth, was meticulous and effective. The second was far too fond of the sound of her own voice. I learned much more from Jon. Hillocks had asked us to prepare a unit for student-teaching—an outline, really—but I decided I might as well plan out the entire thing. So I turned in 200 pages. I don't think he'd ever received that many pages before. He sent them back with instructions to revise. "In an outline form," he reminded me.

As a student teacher, I was still a mess, but I gained a

better grasp of managing time, both within an individual class period and during a lesson sequence. I made my first parent phone call (to the parent of the student who was the subject of my unsuccessful educational psychology paper).[30] I learned about how to give students choices when it came to writing about literature after I spent a weekend or so reading fifty or so pretty similar essays on how American settlers and American Indians have different views on land. I got better organized, to keep up with make-up assignments for those who were absent or had missed their first opportunity. I learned to insist that the students put their chairs back in the boundaries that Mr. Nemeth had taped to the floor. He taught me a lot about record keeping. My focus was definitely on content. There was little time to form relationships. Compared to the Harvard School, there were so many students. It was hard to keep up. I wasn't discouraged; I was enjoying the challenge. Like the rest of my colleagues who were student teaching, I was also exhausted. Hillocks came to observe and said I was doing well with "intransigent" students. I had to look up what the word meant.

Given that I was about to finish my graduate program, it was now my wife's turn to pursue her graduate studies. She had found the person she wanted to work with at the University of Pittsburgh, so I'd opened a file on how to find a job in Pittsburgh. I was sitting at the table I'd adopted as

---

30 The parent would later come in to watch her son in class. In the hall, as she and I were waiting to enter (and before the students arrived), she wondered out loud whether she should just beat him in front of his classmates. I think I managed a feeble protest against such a choice; she did not beat him. I'm not sure my protest had anything to do with her restraint.

my desk in the English office when the phone rang. It was Kirsten. She asked a question that would determine the next seven years of our life:

"Where's Vanderbilt?"

I covered the phone and asked the same question of the English office. Someone said, "Near Nashville." Kirsten was calling from a conference she was attending with her prospective professor, who was then at the University of Pittsburgh, and he'd told her that he was going to take a job at Vanderbilt and that he was still happy to have her as a student if she wanted to follow. It was only fair; it was her turn. We were going to follow. I threw away the Pittsburgh file and started one for Nashville.

We were moving to Nashville, the self-proclaimed "Buckle of the Bible Belt," and I had no job. I had one epic phone interview, though, and the principal and I seemed to be simpatico. I recall pacing in the front hall of our apartment, adrenaline surging through me when the principal announced that he had just one more question. I expected it to be, "Would you like the job?" Or, "When can you come visit so we can meet in person?" I could not have been more wrong. The question was: "Do you accept Jesus Christ as your Lord and Savior?"

It would not be the last unusual interview question I got in Nashville. With little sense of the city's geography or the school system, I scheduled a series of interviews there during a visit arranged for us to find a place to live and me to find a job.

At one school, I glanced at the school's mission statement moments before I was called back for an interview. It contained the usual blather about "well-rounded" and "citizens of the world" and "lifelong learning." And it also promised to teach its students how to have a "healthy sexual lifestyle." As I turned around to ask Kirsten where in the heck we were, I was called back for the interview. Therefore, it was no surprise that I was completely unprepared for the question: "What would you do if you came across two students having sex?" We did notice the barbed wire around the parking lot and building on the way out. I learned later that it was a school for first-time teen sex offenders.

A school I was interested in kept me waiting for a long time with only a dated *Town & Country* magazine for company. When I was finally called into the principal's office, she asked, before I even sat down, "Do you know another word for 'diversity' that has the same number of letters?" I remember contemplating making a run for it. This same principal asked me what I'd bring to a faculty potluck[31] (pasta salad—lame, I know, but I figured that I'd have to follow through if I got the job) and grilled me about volleyball strategy, a sport I only knew about from watching it at the Olympics.

I also had an interview at Wharton Arts Magnet Middle School. I was struck at the time by how much the teachers seemed eager to persuade me to work there. I learned later that it was less about wanting me there than antipathy toward the candidate put forth by the quirky assistant principal. The teachers must have won the argument; this would be the job I'd get, though not until the third or fourth day of the professional development week.

One of the things every teacher is eager to see before the

---

31 Food was a big issue in Nashville schools. More on faculty potlucks when I finally get a job.

school year begins is a student roster.[32] I was standing in the hall looking mine over when one name struck me: Billie Jayne Thompson. "My God," I thought. "I really am in the South."

Billie Jayne was in the second row center on the first day and she soon put her hand up. Since I was pretty sure, unlike at the Harvard School, that I'd already mentioned my name, I wondered what her question could possibly be.

"Are you Jewish?" she asked.

It was only fair. I'd stereotyped her first.

To this day, it absolutely stuns me how lucky I was to fall into such a great team of teachers for one of two times in my life. I think part of the reason is that we all knew that we had a terrible principal, so we looked to each other to solve problems rather than to her. We all recognized our strengths and what we could each contribute. I think it also helped that we had a grade level hall. Geography matters. We could easily bump into each other and have those small and short conversations that make the days flow more easily.

And we supported each other. When a teacher had a student pulled out to be arrested for having a gun in his locker, I went in to relieve her so she could catch her breath. When a colleague had her water break, she turned to a colleague to drive her to the hospital. These are extreme examples, but they illustrate my point. Our hall felt unified, harmonious.

---

32 In fact, while I was procrastinating, I saw that my principal had sent us the list for this year with all of the necessary qualifications (students are still registering, withdrawing, etc.). My first period class has ten students. I have one other section of seventeen and the others are in the low twenties. No major complaints, but I hope the first period class gains a few more students. I am all in favor of small class sizes, but that might be a bit too small.

All those kinds of good things you can feel when you are in sync with your colleagues. And the students knew it, too.

Things were better in the classroom for me, though I still didn't feel competent or confident. One of the first things I was handed when I got to the district was the list of books I could not teach. One was a book I'd used during student teaching, *I Know Why the Caged Bird Sings* by Maya Angelou. Shortly after the year started, I went to the library to look at all of the books on the list. One was hard to find. It turned out that that book, *The Baby Uggs Were Hatching*, a story about the reproductive process, was in the children's section. When I got home and opened *Love Story*, another book from the forbidden list, I saw that someone had crossed out all of the mentions of "God" in the expletives.

I tried to approach the classes thematically, as I'd been taught in graduate school. I let the students choose the books and ordered them accordingly. I've always had a hard time using textbooks in English classes. I don't mind picking and choosing excerpts, but who wants to carry that thing back and forth to read from it? I saw a presentation by the frenetic Jeffrey Wilhelm, and his book, *You Gotta BE the Book,* opened my eyes to how I could balance my desire to be creative with the requirement to attend to the standards.

At this time, Kirsten was at the Peabody School of Education at Vanderbilt. That meant she worked with professors who had student teachers. And these student teachers needed a place to student teach, so I agreed to host a few. I think this is one of the few parts of teacher education that ought to be preserved, at least in some form. If it's well-executed, it hearkens back to the apprenticeship model of learning a trade. I learned a great deal from the two people who served as my cooperating teachers, even if I thought one was particularly poor at her job. The other, though, is someone I still think of today. Though I thought putting tape marks on the floor to indicate where the chair legs ought to be was a bit much, he was impeccably organized. His lesson plans, his grade book, his handouts, his desk—they were all a marvel and worthy of imitation.

I am not sure at this point what, if anything, I knew about my first student teacher, but it didn't take me long to figure out that he was pretty proud of his long hair and his earring. And I was not completely shocked that I had to tell him, in no uncertain terms, that going over to the home of a middle school girl to tutor her *while her parents were not home* was not acceptable. The science teacher down the hall had a student teacher tell her (after she'd offered some advice) that cooperating teachers were meant to be seen and not heard. I suggested that she call the professor in question and have the student removed. The last I saw of my student teacher (after he'd been hired) was a quick interview spot with him in which he proclaimed the righteousness of the union in a right-to-work state.

In any event, I believe I got a reputation as a home for the troubled teacher candidates. The following year I had an older candidate assigned to me who was, to say the least, erratic and emotional. She both swore at me and wept during one meeting. As a friend said to me, "Crying is good; swearing is not." I don't think I ever knew whether she found a job. It would be some time before I'd agree to host another student-teacher.

***

As I settled into the job at Wharton, I continued to experiment. I received a great deal of useful professional development about how to use arts in the classroom. I even learned all of the words to a song by the Judds. I took students on an annual field trip to the Country Music Hall of Fame because in the middle of the tour they'd have a brief concert featuring a local musician who'd taken student lyrics that I'd submitted ahead of time and set a few of them to music. The student who wrote "Get A Life.Com" is still very serious about his music. I've lost track of the student who wrote "I Apologize," but I can still remember some of the words.

I was still adjusting to life in the South. There was only one other Jewish person in the building, the assistant principal. As an arts magnet school, we were often given free tickets to shows that were travelling through town. At one point, *Fiddler on the Roof* was coming, and if I'd charged every student and teacher a nickel for questions they asked me about it in advance, I could have doubled my salary. But we didn't get to go because of a snow day.[33]

Wharton also introduced me to the tradition of faculty potlucks. A fellow teacher knocked on my door one day asking what I planned to bring. I hated interruptions then

---

33 Snow days in Nashville were surreal. Kirsten once drove me to school on a snow day because we hadn't even thought to check the news first. A colleague and I played tennis in shorts on another. The radio would carry announcements about which Kroger grocery stores were running out of milk, bread, etc..

(and still do),[34] so I just said the first thing that came to mind that I knew we had ingredients for—hummus. Over the next few days before the potluck, several teachers approached me cautiously and asked me, "What's hue-muss?" I took it as a challenge. My monthly contribution was going to be my[35] contribution to their Jewish education.

I didn't know that it was a tradition for students to bring their teachers Christmas presents on the last day before the break. One shy student had to be prodded by his mother to hand me a gift bag that was decorated with Jewish stars. "He was so proud that he remembered you were Jewish," she said. I thanked them and assured them that I would not have taken offense. I set the bag with the rest of the gifts—most of them food—and didn't look inside until I got home. What was inside the bag with the Jewish stars? A Santa mug. I think I still have it.

There were two trials going on during my Wharton years that got everyone's attention: the O.J. Simpson trial and a local trial to restrict the teaching of evolution in Tennessee.[36] This prompted a unit that involved studying the play *Inherit the Wind*. To get a sense of things before we began, I asked the students about their own beliefs. In one class, twenty-two out of twenty-six students did not believe in evolution. I was,

---

34 Dana Goldstein has an excellent example of how American these interruptions are in her excellent book, *The Teacher Wars*.

35 I should say "our" as Kirsten generally took care of the cooking. My effort at rugelach was a flour-y disaster.

36 If the editorial pages of the local newspaper count as evidence, there were still some Tennesseans fighting the Civil War. Sorry, strike that—the War of Northern Aggression.

shall we say, surprised. The science teacher was probably wise to decline my offer to collaborate.

Now that I think of it, 1994 was quite a year. O.J. Simpson was acquitted. Princess Diana died. Kurt Cobain committed suicide. I had no idea that such things would have so much of an impact on my students. To this day, I still don't think I understand the intensity of their reaction to the O.J. Simpson case.

***

My advisor at Chicago had encouraged us to join the National Council of Teachers of English (NCTE), and so I did. During my first conference, I had transformative sessions with Jeffrey Wilhelm and Bill Ayers. It was an amazing experience.

I was on the local host committee for the next year's conference, held at Opryland in Nashville. They gave me a pink cowboy hat[37] and told me to help people find their sessions. Since I need a GPS to get to the bathroom in the middle of the night, I was not very good at my task. Opryland was challenging even for those who are not navigationally impaired. Aside from being able to direct people to the Andrew Jackson room, I am pretty sure I was not helpful at all. Still, doing a shift or two saved me some money. That this conference predated social media saved me some embarrassment. As far as I know, there are no pictures of me in that hat.

I got better at navigating the NCTE program— I found myself attracted to a mix of practical sessions and

---

37 Luckily, this was pre-social media.

philosophical ones and always had a second choice in case the first didn't work out. I had to gather the courage to be able to walk out of a session. The conferences eventually became too big for me, and I found other professional organizations. Still, NCTE was a good entry point, and Hillocks was right to encourage our professional affiliation. I even managed to publish an article or two with them.

For what it's worth, if you are reading this and you are a young teacher, I do strongly encourage you to get involved with some professional organization. I think NCTE made me realize the breadth and depth of the English teaching profession and how many thinkers and practitioners are out there. Keep looking; you'll find your home.

I learned a lot from my experience at Wharton. I figured out that middle school was probably not the best place for me. I learned the value of a strong set of colleagues. I learned how to infuse arts into the curriculum. I learned how important it was to work with a principal who made sense to me. I also learned how much it helped to have good relationships with students and their families.

I'm not sure when or why or how it happened, but I finally felt real. I learned that I was a teacher.

Rant: Floating

I understand the logistical necessity of having teachers share classrooms and that once in a while, teachers have to share classrooms and teach in two (or more) classrooms. I am well aware that teachers who speak of classrooms as "*my* classroom" are wrong.

The classroom belongs to the school. And since most teachers are pack rats, the longer a teacher stays in one space, the harder it is to dislodge them if it's their turn to float. Often, schedulers will just work around them rather than dealing with their objections. I've even known a half-time teacher to throw a fit because someone was using "his" classroom *when he wasn't even there*. And, as with all other things, he made himself obnoxious enough to deal with that most people just conceded rather than argue with him. But I don't want anyone to forget that this floating business is very, very hard.

At my current school, when everyone on our staff floats no one has to switch classrooms in the three-minute break between classes. I have my planning period and lunch to make the adjustment. Here's the thing, though—since I buy most of my supplies, do I have to buy a set for each room or do I get a cart or something to move things between rooms? And if I forget something that means a sprint between rooms. And it also means never feeling comfortable, never feeling settled.

I remember reading once about the morale problem with 911 operators in Detroit. Everyone shared cubicles so no one was allowed to leave things or put up pictures or make the space their own in any way. Now I can put up posters or whatever, but I can't be there to make sure stuff on my desk doesn't get touched. (And no, I don't have a desk in an office.)

Another complication of sharing is the arrangement of the rooms themselves. I've had to float into science classrooms with their immovable tables. Right now, I share one of my rooms with a new teacher. She's great. And she wants the chairs and tables in islands or clusters angled around the room. I hate that. I don't like people to have their backs to me (at least at the beginning), and it has made it harder for me to learn names. And I also don't want to reset the classroom when I get in there and then reset it at the end of the day when I'm finished. I know I can train students to do it, but that would eat into my time. Simply put, I want the room my way. But I will only vent here for now. I am trying to make her comfortable.

I have great roommates and, with one exception, have always had great roommates. And I've tried to be a good roommate. But people have different work styles, attitudes about playing music, making phone calls, casual conversation, etc.. I have long fantasized about going to the district office and stepping into the office of some important person to say, "Sorry, I need to work here for an hour. You can work over there." One day, maybe. . .

5
Hume-Fogg High School
Nashville, TN

Somewhere during my third year at Wharton, a pattern started that would persist throughout my career. People had started to leave. I started to get restless, especially with our principal. An opportunity to transfer to the Hume-Fogg Academic Magnet School came up, and I took it.

Hume-Fogg is regularly listed as one of the top public high schools in the country. The principal, a legend, was in her thirty-seventh and final year. When she asked me about books I'd like to teach, I gave her my list and she said she hated *The Crucible*. Still, I got the job. Initially, I hung out with a great social studies teacher, and we talked about forming a charter school. The concept of charter schools intrigued me then. I still think they could have worked, but as with many things in education, the idea exploded and got diluted and abused very quickly.[38]

I should probably explain why there were so many magnet schools in the district. Nashville was, almost fifty years after the *Brown v Board of Education* verdict, still under court order to desegregate the city's schools. I wouldn't exactly call fifty years "all deliberate speed." Every year, there would be a photo of empty chairs at the math and science magnet school (named, not coincidentally, after Martin Luther King), and the tale of white students who had been admitted there but then told they'd

---

38 See Multiple Intelligences, Inventive Spelling, Writing Across the Curriculum, technology, etc.

have to go elsewhere because not enough black students applied.

My experience at Wharton was that I could generally draw a line down the center of the classroom, and you'd find white students on one side and black students on the other. The few who "crossed over" were generally the most mature. And while you can force students to get on a bus together if they want specialized arts programs or the best academic program, you can't force them to socialize with each other. It was even difficult to assign group projects to be completed outside of class. These were not students who spent time at each other's houses.

It was around the fourth day of school at Hume-Fogg when the office put through a call to my classroom. It was Kirsten; we'd been robbed. Someone had taken our VCR. Everyone, including the principal, was very supportive. This helped me begin to become comfortable at the school. A few days later, we were discussing Jonathan Swift's "A Modest Proposal." I gave the assignment that the essay screams out for—write your own modest proposal. A young man, definitely bound for the military, wrote something, I can't remember what, but his mother wrote the principal and said—and this I can remember—that I was teaching her son to think "outside the bounds of civilized minds."[39] I waited for the principal to comment. She said, "I knew you were good." I was in love.

Hume-Fogg's English department was close knit, and I never really found my way into it. I was not at the school long enough to settle in, but it was a good year. I relished the energetic intelligence of the students. I learned a lot;

---

39 This would rate as my favorite compliment for close to twenty years.

my toolbox continued to grow.[40] The district celebrated the members of my cohort who had earned National Board Certification. I was invited to a school board meeting to be recognized. I almost didn't make it because I locked my keys in my car when I first stopped by the softball practice I was supposed to be running.

But despite the positive beginning, the atmosphere at Hume-Fogg was not always welcoming. I was assigned tasks outside the classroom for which I was either under- or overqualified. I grew frustrated with colleagues who mistook "challenging" for " more." Fifty homework problems for math is not challenging; it's just a lot.

Softball was a bright spot. It occasioned another great interaction with my principal. For some reason, we were allowed to set our own departure times for sports events. The school is downtown; all sports events, including practices, required a commute. She thought I'd left too early for one game. There was a note in my box the next day telling me so. It concluded with, "This is my version of shared decision making. I made a decision and shared it with you." I laughed. That was fine with me. There was no meeting. There was clarity. This was my kind of principal.

But the best interaction with her was the occasion of my most epic plagiarism case. A student submitted an extra credit assignment on the movie *Pleasantville*, and it was plagiarized. Rather than flag it to the appropriate authorities or call out the student directly, I buried it. Maybe I thought she'd figure it out. Maybe I just didn't know how to handle it. But my

---

40 Wow, that is a mixed metaphor. But I think you know what I mean.

lack of a response was definitely a mistake.

Soon after, I became pretty sure she'd plagiarized a regular assignment. This time, I called her up after class and went through the usual questions. *Do you know what plagiarism is? Did you get any help with this?* She was calm and polite and insisted it was her original work. I left that day not sure what to do. I hadn't been able to find proof yet.

Her mother called me at home that night.[41] She was, she yelled, a private investigator by trade, and I had no proof, and how dare I ask her daughter about plagiarism. Now I knew what I had to do next.

At Hume-Fogg, I parked on the first floor and the main office was on the second floor. When I went to sign in, I ran into the librarian, gave her the paper, and asked her if she could find the source. I think I talked to maybe one person, and by the time I arrived at the door of my classroom on the fourth floor, she had the student's paper and its source. Word-for-word plagiarism. It was conference time.

The school had a student court. It was supposed to be anonymous, but when the announcement came over the intercom for the student court to assemble, everyone knew who was involved. At the initial parent conference, I was given some options, and I chose to let the student court decide. The student made her case while I waited outside. Then we switched places. The court found her guilty, and her punishment included writing an essay on

---

41 I gave out my home phone number then. I give out my cell phone now. It's just easier.

plagiarism that she would have to submit in order to take the semester exam.

The exam day came and she handed me the essay as she walked into my classroom. I was sensitive enough to try to be casual about it. I got everyone set up, answered some questions, and then sat down to glance at the plagiarism essay. And, sure enough, it was plagiarized. A few sentences into the first page, the phrase, "In the next chapter" appeared. I read it all the way to the end, perhaps hoping for some kind of ironic conclusion. Nothing. When the designated relief person came to give me a break, I brought the essay down to the principal and offered my opinion. She must have agreed. When I returned to check in after the exam, she was on the phone with the student's mother. The parent must have said something about being offended by the accusation. I heard the principal's response. So did everyone in the office, and everyone on Music Row: "In thirty-seven years, I've never had any student do something this stupid."

That wasn't my only legal issue that year. I was driving home from school during that same stretch of semester exams when I saw that some of our students had been in a car accident. I pulled over, discovered there were no serious injuries and identified myself to the paramedic. We both knew what *in loco parentis* meant.[42] I said that they were all going to the emergency room. I drove the final few blocks back to our apartment building, walked back to the scene of the accident, and got into the ambulance with the students. Three of them were cleared shortly after we arrived there, and they were promptly

---

42 And if you don't, you should.

picked up by their parents. The fourth, a female, was placed on twenty-four-hour concussion watch. She told me her mother was out of town and she had no interest in contacting her father. I called my principal for advice. She told me to take the student home with me. I called my wife. I was not going to be home alone with a female student. The next day, the principal called Child and Family Services, and the student was furious with me. I tried to explain that I'd had no choice, but she didn't want to hear it.

***

The end of that school year also brought some tension. I'd volunteered to chaperone the prom. This time, there was a different call over the intercom, not from the student court, but for the chaperones. We were to report to the conference room. We were told that a student who had been expelled earlier in the year had been profiled as a potential school shooter.[43] It was the year of the Columbine shooting. I remembered a valuable lesson I'd learned that day. I had been prepared to lead the students in a discussion about the shooting when a reliable student said, "Can we just have our normal day?" Everything in the world outside was chaotic; that student wanted "normal" and no one in the class argued with him.

When I got to the conference room, we were told told that as prom chaperones we needed to keep an eye out for the expelled student. We received a small photo. I wondered what I was supposed to do if I saw him. I knew his ex-girlfriend; she had red hair. I called my parents before I left for the prom,

---

43 See Epilogue.

though I didn't tell them why. Both parts of that seemed like the right thing to do.

The prom was on the eighth floor of some building I can't remember. Some people got the job of sitting across from the elevators and helping students sign in, collect their goodies, etc. I wondered what they were supposed to do if the elevator door opened and they saw the boy in the picture. I didn't get that job. I spent most of the evening following my student, his ex-girlfriend. Her red hair made that easier. The expelled student never showed up. He didn't show up for the school's traditional processional from the school to the graduation location downtown, the new hockey arena. But we were told that the police snipers on the roofs of various downtown buildings were keeping an eye out for him. That may have been the longest five blocks of my life.

Around that time, Kirsten came back to our apartment as I was marking essays. She saw what I was doing and said, "Can I ask you an important question later?" Nervous, I put my pen in the margin of the essay to mark my place and told her to ask it now. If you had given me a million guesses, I would not have been able to predict what she'd ask.

"Do you want to move to London?"

Her advisor, the one who had made me throw away my Pittsburgh file in favor of a Nashville one, was now considering a job at King's College, London, and had assured Kirsten that there would be a place for her there as well. We had a long talk and decided to go. I must have gotten back to the essays at some point. When I finally returned the one essay I'd been grading when I was interrupted, the student asked me why there was so much scribbling on one particular session of her work.

Rant: Advisories

I get the reason for advisories, I really do, especially in middle school. Schools want someone looking after the "whole child." Parents want a contact point at the school. And, of course, there's a tremendous amount of paperwork required to administer a school, and it's easiest to run it through an advisory. (The alternative is inevitably English class, another source of frustration.)

Here's the thing, though. Absolutely no one in the world grows up and says, "I want to be a middle school advisor." We want to be teachers. Maybe we even want to be middle school teachers. (I don't anymore.) But we don't go into the profession to be advisors in any kind of official capacity. Some people are naturally good at it. More power to them. But we are not given any classes about it in graduate school, and we are, at best, given binders full of someone else's curriculum, often pockmarked from being copied too many times.

So if you want me to manage a portion of the administrative load with a small group of randomly selected students, fine. If you want me to take attendance first thing in the morning, also fine. If you want me to just hang out with a group of students for a set period of time, well, that seems like a waste of time. What is the goal of advisory or homeroom or whatever you want to call it? If the goal is to have the students have one adult on their side, well, I think most generally find that adult themselves. Failing that, place advisees with advisors deliberately—not always easy at first, I know.

Clearly, I'm not a natural. I had told my advisory at Hume-Fogg that they were welcome to come to advisory and hang out, but I didn't really care. All I needed was for them to wave and let me know they were present. Then a French teacher accosted me and said one of my advisees was hanging out in the hallway near her door and engaging in too many public displays of affection with his girlfriend and that I needed to talk to him. I didn't know I was leaving at that point, so I was trying to be a good colleague. I gave up trying to be serious about it roughly eight seconds into the conversation and ended up asking if they'd consider shifting their PDA sessions out of the sightlines of that particular teacher.

Other times, I would try to take my role seriously. I had one advisee who missed the first ten weeks of school. When he returned after our fall break and was picked up by the police a few days later, I spent a lot of time and energy trying to get him out from under the clutches of the juvenile justice system. When people would ask me why, my only response was that he was my advisee. He'd been randomly put on my list, so I was responsible for him.[44]

---

44 I eventually did help get him out; he got himself put back in.

6
The American School in London (ASL)
London, UK

Finding work in a new city—let alone a new country—is no easy task. But for the first time, I had a job prior to our move to the UK. I was going to teach in the eighth grade at the American School in London (ASL), located in St. John's Wood near Abbey Road.[45]

Given that I've moved around so much, I should share that my general approach to trying to find a job in a new city is to spray and pray. That is, I paper the city with my information, and follow up on any leads, no matter how small. I had this notion that I would teach in London's equivalent of public schools. Without much knowledge about or regard for geography, I wasted a lot of postage to no good effect. I began to stack up my rejection notices, along with a fair number of course listings, often highlighted. If I would just take this and that course, I was told, then I could be considered. But I was in no mood to go into any classroom as a student.[46]

What saved me is that Kirsten discovered that an officemate had spent some time at ASL, so I applied and

---

45 Yes, I walked across that intersection. With shoes on.

46 Before we left London three years later, they were recruiting teachers from all over the Commonwealth. Some schools even resorted to closing on Fridays because they could not find a way to be fully staffed. I'm not sure how closing Fridays helped that situation. Regardless, I admit I felt just a wee bit of malicious glee.

included the insider information the officemate provided. Having been ignored the first time I applied, I was suddenly an attractive candidate. After a good phone interview, I was invited to visit in person. We went in April of that year and I missed a few softball games, but I got the job. I was pretty excited. Maybe it was just relief.

Just as the move from Chicago to Nashville had meant adjusting to a new culture, so did the move from Nashville to London. The US and England, the head of school at ASL said, are two countries "separated by the same language." We secured a small granny flat, or apartment, thanks to my mother and waited (and waited and waited) for our life to arrive in boxes.

The commute was easy. I rode the red #82 bus, on the top when I could, all the way to St. John's Wood. This afforded me ample reading time, and I needed it. It is always difficult to begin at a new school or even in a new class and teach someone else's curriculum. This challenge was compounded at ASL because the guardian of that curriculum was also the partner of the middle school principal.[47]

My first lesson in the kind of students I'd be working with came on the first day. In addition to teaching eighth grade English, I was also assigned to teach eighth grade American history. During the first class, two hands went up. The first student asked me where we'd be starting. When I told her we would begin with the events leading up to the Constitution, she said, "What's the Constitution?" Another student, as new

---

47 The presence of couples at independent schools deserves its own book. It certainly plagued me here and in Minnesota.

to the school as I was, groaned and said, "I did that last year."

Many of the students were third culture kids. They were moved around Europe and elsewhere at the whim of their parents and their parents' employers. A few years later, I'd run into one of my students at the airport. I was going to Nice, and he was on the same flight. He did not look happy. When I asked him why, he said, "I just want to stay in England with my friends." I felt a strange kind of sadness for him.

Before I'd gotten to dive too deeply into the curriculum, we had our eighth grade field trip: a bus trip to Wales for our advisories to bond by attending the first Outward Bound Center. So I got on the bus, or "coach," with my randomly selected advisory, and we headed to Wales, land of the Scrabble-friendly language. The only movies that our students could agree on for their entertainment featured Adam Sandler. This would hold true for the next two trips as well. Good for Adam Sandler and our students. Not so good for my sanity.

It proved to be the first of many school experiences there and elsewhere that no one could explain to me. We seemed to be going, that first year, because that's what the eighth grade did and there were some vague hopes that this one-time massive expenditure of money would unify these advisories of ten to twelve students who didn't really spend much time as a group except for in Wales and if they showed up for their advisory's date for the service project.

I didn't really know what I was doing there. I tried to be supportive of my group's guide, but she told me I was too involved, so I went off, with a few other advisors, to have tea and scones in this small Welsh village. I remember sitting next to our huge Australian rugby coach. I bought a mug. It was a surreal experience.

***

One thing you should know about me is that I ask questions. And I generally demonstrate my low emotional intelligence by not really caring how I ask them. In short, I'm rude, though sometimes it's not on purpose. I've generally been able to live with that perception and reputation, at least until I flirted with administrative roles. A friend in London once suggested that I get that T-shirt that says, "I Have Enough Friends.'

I have never been in teaching because of the adults. If I didn't think a project was right for the students, I said so. Repeatedly. I often able to make some small changes, but the status quo is a powerful thing.

The biggest factor in my experience at ASL was money. People treated it like Monopoly money. Staff dinners were ridiculously extravagant. Teachers received gifts from parents that were just stunning. One teacher, in fact the teacher whose name I'd dropped in my cover letter to the school, was disappointed at receiving what probably amounted to over $400 in theater gift certificates. She had expected much more. Knowing that I was a theater fan, she offered to sell them to me. I declined.

That kind of entitlement just dominated the place. Teachers complaining that breaks weren't long enough, that they were told to do too much, or just complaining in general. There was no sense of perspective. Some had been there too long; others had swallowed the Kool-Aid too fast.

Early in my first year, my principal was in charge of a conference in the city. A presenter bailed at the last minute and she sent an email around to ask if anyone would take the spot. Since I was still in my "I need to be impressive" mode, I offered, and the presentation, on censorship, went well. She must have been pleased because she offered me a handout shortly after I emerged from the session and asked me if I wanted to present at another conference as well. I read it and was nodding along until I got to the bottom.

"You know this is in Beijing?" I said.

"We'll send you," she said. Just like that. I decided that being at a school that has money was not always going to be a bad thing. And so I went.

And that wasn't the only all-expenses paid trip. We used Nancie Atwell's Writers' Workshop in the eighth grade, and I saw that she was on a speaking tour. Off I went to New York City. Then to San Francisco for NCTE. And if I wanted materials for my classroom, there was no process, no form, and no limit. I just bought it and was reimbursed.

The students too. One year, a bus got stuck at the top of the hill at the Outward Bound Center in Wales. I muttered something to a student whose parent, I knew, was very wealthy. "Maybe your Dad could get us a plane to fly us out of here?"

"I'll call him," she said. After an overly long pause, I told her she could put her cell phone away.

In coaching, too, extravagance ruled the day. We received absurd per diems; many coaches abused them. Little attention was paid to record-keeping by our then athletic director. I don't know why I hadn't thought of it before I started to coach, but as an American school, we played other schools in the consortium. While there were two others in England, a US military school, and a few local schools we competed with, most of the time, we went to other countries to play. Because of its location, I think I ended up going to Brussels close to a dozen times.

∗∗∗

I continued teaching American history my second year at ASL, and this meant I was teaching during the contentious 2000 Bush-Gore-Nader election. My father, a resident of Washington D.C., was kind enough to send me the special afternoon editions of *The Washington Post* on a regular basis. Things moved even faster than the Internet. I had a lesson planned on the Nader-trader effort,[48] but events moved too fast for me. And to the dozens of people who sent me the oh-so-hysterical email about the Queen being willing to take the US back because we couldn't seem to self-govern effectively, thank you. It was funny every single time.

At the start of my third year, the school building was undergoing renovations, so we pushed our first day to September 10. September 10, 2001. That means, with the time difference, we learned of the terrorist attacks on the afternoon of our second day of school. The eighth grade assistant waved me into her office

---

48 Nader was trying to get enough votes for matching funds in the future. People were offering to vote for him in states where the outcome was certain in exchange for votes for Gore in states that were still up in the air. By the time I arrived at the school the next morning, such transactions had been declared to be in violation of commerce laws and the websites had been shut down.

and said, "A plane just flew into one of the World Trade Center towers in New York. They think it's terrorism."

It was just so far out of the realm of my vocabulary that I couldn't really take in the news. The assistant reminded me that one of our teachers, a wonderful teacher, had family in the area of the Twin Towers. I asked her to walk the teacher to a private phone and then send her home. I just wanted to make it to the end of the day. We got all of the students out of there, and I rounded up contact numbers for the eighth grade staff. And waited.

I am not sure why I stayed at school so long. I tried to reach my wife whose office was located in the center of London near the densely populated Waterloo Station.[49] I tried to contact my family. My father lived in D.C., and my mother in a suburb just outside of the city in Maryland. I connected with my sister, who encouraged me to go home.

I finally went home and turned on the television. Kirsten came home, and we watched together for a while. And then we turned it off and didn't watch anymore. To be across an ocean from those you love and all that you find familiar at such a time was to be unmoored. The ocean felt like it had gotten bigger.

The decision was made that staff should arrive at the normal time the next day, but that students would be expected in the afternoon. The school had found people to help us help the students, all of whom were far from home (and some of whom had New York as their base) to find some way to negotiate this, this thing that had happened.

I don't remember much of what was said at that

---

49 It is featured in one of the Jason Bourne movies.

morning meeting. I remember asking my advisory to write or draw and that one student broke down crying. I remember that another teacher, notoriously tone deaf, had the male students in his advisory crowding around his computer to watch the video of the planes being crashed into the towers, so I asked the guidance counselor to check on him. He closed the door on her.

We found our way into the school year, though the attacks colored our daily lives. Later that year, plane crashed somewhere in New York or New Jersey, and the teacher from New York asked me about it, and I tried to gently remind her that sometimes, before the attack, planes crashed, and people were hurt, investigations happened, and we went on. I'm not sure she believed me. Some of my advisees wanted to raise money for the Red Cross, but the Red Cross was having some internal issues, so that became a contentious conversation. The opponents were divided by the ocean. The British teacher wanted the money to go elsewhere. The American teacher pushed for the Red Cross. I cast the deciding vote and said that we would honor the students' wishes. The money went to the Red Cross.

***

At ASL, I started down a path that I would not emerge from for almost fifteen years. We needed a "team leader" for the eighth grade, and it sort of fell to me. The transience of the staff was such that I was already one of the more experienced people in eighth grade, and people seemed to think I was a natural successor. So I signed on the dotted line.

I don't think I was the best team leader. I tried to

make more of the role than was probably there. I observed classes and wrote up my notes. I was sometimes rude or intimidating or something and would put people off. One of my regular troubles is that I am not always very adept at recognizing the impact my words and tone can have on others. The teacher from New York would later write in a recommendation for me: "What I like about Charles is that if you tell him you disagree or that you think he did something wrong, he'll think about it. Then he'll come back to you and either apologize or try to explain his thinking again." Not all of the teachers were so generous.

I tried to connect through theater. I sought to arrange evenings out with one or two teachers at a time. I sought to make the Outward Bound experience more meaningful by having the coordinator from Wales come to the school in advance to talk through both pedagogical and practical things with the eighth grade team. The day before we went, and this was, if you recall, October of 2001, the principal asked if I had a plan. "A plan for what?" I asked. "In case something happens here and you all can't come back for a while." Twenty-four hours later I had a plan.

I tried to make our meetings more focused, more worthwhile. I'm not sure where I got it from, but I implemented a "Discuss/Decide/Inform" frame for each agenda item. I tried hard to negotiate the tension around the music classes and the tension with the Modern Language department.

I was finally "in the room where it happens"[50] and so it would drive me crazy when people would resort to the cliché

---

50 *Hamilton*

of, "This needs to be a bigger conversation." I would think, and occasionally and generally unsubtly express that this *was* the bigger conversation, that we were the people in charge of our various slices of the school, and that *we* therefore had the authority to make changes. Now that I think about it, though, I think people would resort to "the bigger conversation" cliché when they weren't getting their way. The message was delivered in what I found to be a typically British passive-aggressive sort of way: "You don't agree with me, so you must not understand. Therefore, we must talk more." In the end, we did so very little. Too many cooks, I think.

I led some efforts that were received well, at least in my memory. A career day. A day filled with Writers' Workshop session from all different perspectives (songwriting, newspaper writing, etc.). I connected well with the eighth grade parents so our back-to-school night was more useful, I was told. I made a sustained effort to shield a math teacher from one set of parents who were berating her over one assignment. These parents would ultimately call me "imperious and arrogant." The teacher would ultimately give me a bottle of Bailey's Irish Cream. Guess who I liked better?

Before we left for England, my mother had given me a wall hanging of sorts. It featured Samuel Johnson and a quotation of his: *A man who is tired of London is tired of life*. It started to make me feel guilty. I was getting tired of London. I was not happy with the leadership role. Kirsten had her own reasons for wanting to move back to the United States. We decided it was time to go.

Someone once wrote, "Money doesn't solve all problems, but very few problems are solved without money." The

American School in London had plenty of money. But with a transient student and teacher population, a lack of curricular oversight (more on this when I describe my role at Blake, which also had a lot of money) cloaked in the guise of being independent, and an erratic teacher evaluation program, the school was incoherent. Outstanding in places, at times, but overall, despite all of the money, kind of a mess. To be fair, the amount of money, though I certainly took advantage of it, made me uncomfortable. I was finished with private schools.

Or so I thought.

Rant: Copiers

Some teachers can do it; I generally can't, though I've gotten better over the years. Fix copiers, I mean. When I run the world,[51] a certain number of people in each building will receive training on how to fix copiers and be on call for such services.

And then there's the topic of paper. Everyone loves the idea of recycled paper. Everyone except the cheap industrial copiers that schools get.

And the scramble for copy paper is absurd. I've yet to be at a school that requires donations of copy paper (or toilet paper, for that matter) from parents, but I can understand how it happens. Like all other teachers I know, I spend a great deal of money on

---

51 A job I'm expecting to start any day now.

supplies for my own classroom, but somehow buying copy paper bothers me the most. There are people who hoard it, carefully removing the five extra sheets they brought with them from their classroom after they've finished their copying. I can't do it. I leave the extra paper behind. I just can't be that petty. When I became **d**epartment **c**hair in Baltimore, I resolved to make the trains run on time. The copier would work, and we would have enough paper. I used to lie to the custodian whenever I saw him making the rounds to deliver paper to various departments. I would tell him that we needed paper, too, and then I'd hide it, so he wouldn't see how much I was accumulating in the English office. I still had to dip into my own supply.

7
Baltimore City College High School
Baltimore, MD

When we decided to come back to the US, we didn't have a particular destination in mind. It came down to Baltimore or Chicago, and Kirsten's Chicago opportunity was amateurishly botched on their end,[52] so Baltimore was the ultimate winner.

As usual, I sprayed a potential district with resumes and even managed a few interviews when we arrived in the spring of 2002. Just after we finished signing the paperwork for our house,[53] my mother called. We figured she wanted to know how everything had gone with the house. Instead, she told me that one school—Baltimore City College High School, one of my top choices—called about an interview. They wanted to see me in an hour.

I remember thinking that the interview went well. Perhaps the time crunch gave me some energy. When asked about my knowledge of the International Baccalaureate program, I exaggerated. OK, I lied. The only thing I really knew about the program is that my brother-in-law had just been expelled from one in New Mexico. The assistant principal would later say that I showed "moxie." I got the job.

---

52 They left a message for her in London *after* we'd flown to Chicago, a flight date that they'd known well in advance.

53 I love my name, but there are times when signing it over and over and over again can become exhausting. Buying a house is one such occasion.

City was a challenge at first because we were working with just one car, and Kirsten, never an early riser,[54] had to commute to Annapolis. I was also told, in the way new teachers are often told such things casually, that I had to have a rather elaborate[55] lesson plans available for inspection each day. So after a long day and a long bus ride home, I would come back to devise a long lesson plan based on a curriculum that was completely new to me. I was also getting a block schedule and teaching in the IB program. It was exhausting.

But I loved the school and its traditions. The third oldest public school in the United States and the alma mater of several members of Congress, City is housed in what is affectionately known as "The Castle on the Hill," so close to the site of the old (and now gone) Memorial Stadium, that the school used to have to close on Opening Day. At one of the opening ceremonies, a student[56] I was just getting to know was introduced to lead the recitation of the Pledge of Allegiance. In Latin. He moved downstage, dressed in his signature technicolors (including his dyed red hair), and was greeted by a tremendous ovation. I was pleasantly confused. I thought the celebration was for this quirky character who knew how to do this quirky thing. But then he began. *And the entire student body joined him.* I was the outsider, one of the few who didn't know the Pledge of Allegiance in Latin. I later learned that it was one of the first things *all* of the students

---

54 She would later relent and drive me into school in the morning.

55 We're talking two pages here, with a dozen or so specified categories.

56 One of the roughly percent of white students at that time.

learned in their required Latin class.[57]

In addition to taking on an IB class for the first time, I was following in the footsteps of a legend, who had left in frustration about the school's leadership. She had been with the seniors I inherited for three years. I knew they (and their parents) would be watching. The first step was to select the books. And that meant reading. A lot.

I took the IB-approved book list to the beautiful Barnes & Noble in the Inner Harbor and started working down the list of authors, many of whom were unfamiliar to me. I had never even heard of Oceanic literature before I saw this list. If living in London had made me more aware of current events in more of the world, it would be this list that would make me more aware of the literature of the world.

The process of selecting books, when an English teacher is lucky enough to have that luxury, is a tricky business. There are many factors in play. How do we choose books that represent a wide range of voices without falling prey to the mile wide/inch deep trap? How do we choose books that will challenge the strongest students and still be accessible to those who struggle with literature? How do we choose books that feature controversial topics and language that may help engage some students but may offend others (and their families)? Some argue, for reasons both pedagogical and lazy, that there should be no class book, but such an option is not available in an IB class. How do we choose books that make

---

57 An excellent idea. Even though there are countless grammar books in the world, Latin, as far as I know, is the most helpful background for understanding the mechanics of how the English language works. I absolutely support the idea of a required ninth grade class. But more on all of this later.

sense *together*, so that the curriculum does not just consist of a parade of books?[58]

There are also cost considerations. Classics, having been reprinted many times and sometimes in the public domain, are generally cheaper. Graphic novels remain incredibly expensive. Choosing the right combination of books proved to be a tricky puzzle, one I relished. I took it to the deadline, even past the deadline. I'd already printed copies of the syllabus and book list when I changed my mind yet again. (What had I been thinking by selecting *Moby Dick*?) I wrote the new selections on the board, and the students, especially the girls, were amused by the title of *A Good Man is Hard to Find*. They were less amused by the title of one of the stories it contains, "The Artificial Nigger." Still, there were no complaints.

The first text, though, was *Hamlet*. While I don't think I suffered the way Daniel Day Lewis did when he played the title role in England, I do think my immersion in the play and supporting materials left me more than a little melancholy. I also had to remember that the IB class was not my only assignment; I was also teaching eleventh grade Honors.[59]

The eleventh grade class was a thematic one: *Man and Monster*.[60] The curriculum there was more in keeping with the way I like to teach. We would later debate why our American Literature class was chronological and British Literature was

---

58 More on this in both this section and the Blake section.

59 Lies, damn lies, and tracking. More coming.

60 *Frankenstein* became the equivalent of *Hamlet* in that class. I still have my much annotated copy I used. I'm afraid to move it for fear it will fall apart.

thematic. I suggested that it was because American teachers tended to know American history and not British history, which I didn't think I was a sufficient reason for the different approaches. I also suggested that our curriculum sort of mapped the coalition in the first Iraq War: America, England, and the world.[61]

These were good conversations to have, and we could have them because we had a good team of teachers and an excellent leader. Part of the reason we had such a good staff was that our principal, disliked by many, was extremely assertive about hiring those he deemed qualified to teach in the city's strongest academic school. He also hired a wonderful department chair, a woman who remains a mentor of mine to this day. She brought coherence to the curriculum and a kind of urgent calmness, as oxymoronic as that might sound, to our work.

As in Nashville, I think our department's unity benefitted from the fact that we were 90 percent all on one hallway. We pushed each other to be better teachers; it only made sense for the IB teachers to work together. We were all generally willing to check our egos at the door and focus on supporting each other and the students. I had this feeling of not wanting to let the team down.

My two IB sections quickly revealed their own personalities. One group was better at discussions and less successful with their writing.[62] The other was pretty much the

---

61 No one laughed. Now that I write it, I'm not sure why I thought it was funny.

62 Now that I think of it, though, two of those students have published books—an English teacher's dream.

reverse. After a time, though, I may have, as teachers are wont to do, turned that into a self-fulfilling prophecy.

I don't have much skin in the game when it comes to designing the ideal schedule. In London, we had A-F days; maybe it was A-G. In other words, we did not speak of Monday as "Monday." It was, for example, an "A" day. That Friday, therefore, was an "E" Day. This made the following Monday an "F" day. Confused? Now imagine being 13. During each sequence, you got one double period for each class and then that class didn't meet the next day. Often, I felt like I would just stay still and teach whoever would show up. In Baltimore, it was just A and B days. Block scheduling has its advantages and disadvantages. I also love the way schools invent time. Nowhere else do times like 9:07 and 11:13 actually mean anything. All I'll say for now about schedules is that the tail should not wag the dog here. That is, schedules should be based on programmatic needs, not available rooms or the number of teachers or anything else. If you start with students in mind, you may have to make some compromises, but you generally make good decisions.

One of the students in my A-day class was a big presence, hard to miss. For pretty much the whole year, he seemed preoccupied, at times almost consumed by . . . something. I tried to give him a few openings to discuss it, but he didn't take them. It was only later that I learned that his father was involved in something in the city that had made headlines, headlines I, unlike almost everyone else in the building, knew nothing about. My immediate reaction was to feel foolish. Why didn't I know? Why didn't anyone tell me? Shortly thereafter, though, I realized it was probably good that I didn't know. Maybe English class was the one place where he knew he wasn't being judged or pitied or anything because of his father's actions.

City also had a longstanding rivalry with the city's math and science magnet school—Baltimore Polytechnic Institute, or Poly.[63] Every Thanksgiving, we played them in football, an event that had moved to the new Ravens stadium. Alumni from both schools showed up in force. Both bands were on full display. It was the world I wanted, the high school world I never had at Georgetown Day, where the notion of cheerleaders was considered an affront to feminism. I thought I'd stay there forever.

***

I'm no fan of tracking in general. I am particularly not a fan when it comes to English. It just doesn't make any sense to me. What is "Honors" English? What does such a distinction really mean? More books? Harder books? Longer essays? Isn't tracking contrary to the diversity that we say we need to make schools (and society, and our natural environment) work well? Could electives be the better route? That is, if I really love English and I want to show colleges that I love it and I'm good at it, what if I filled my elective slots with English credits?

I say all this as preface to one piece of feedback I received from one of my eleventh grade IB students. He told me one day, "You teach this like an IB class." My response: "You're

---

63 Ta-Nehisi Coates is, I believe, an alum. See *The Beautiful Struggle* and *Between the World and Me*.

just as smart as they are; you just chose a different class."
Maybe such a response would not meet with Carol Dweck's
approval (and no longer meets with mine), but he said it on
the way out of class, and we've already seen that I'm not too
golden-tongued when I'm in a hurry. But the essence of what
I believe is in my response. I teach what my experience tells
me the students need in preparation for college. The only
difference is that in the IB classes, I taught to the tests.

I am aware that "teaching to the test" is anathema to
many of us, a practical necessity for some, and a great idea for
others.[64] But I think the IB assessments[65] are good, external
measures of a students' ability. The oral commentary, though
incredibly time consuming, exhausting, and challenging,
really does show what a student knows. The two external
written assignments at the time were equally challenging.
The first required an analysis of a previously unseen passage.
The students could choose from poetry or prose. One year,
they could choose a passage from *Life of Pi*, which doesn't
fit into either category. The second asked students to write a
response to a generic question. An example—Stories either
end by closing up or opening out. Comment."—using the
texts studied in class.

I studied the rubric carefully. According to the guide,
students were rewarded for a "personal response." So all that
first year I taught students to find a place to make a personal
connection. It turned out, however, that "personal response"

---

64 Though if you're still reading, maybe you're re-thinking this.

65 At least as they were given in 2002-2008

actually meant "original response."[66] In other words, IB was sending the message that if everyone interpreted a text in the same way, they would infer that it was the teacher's interpretation. Needless to say, my students extremely personal essays were not what IB was looking for. So as I went on, I pushed original interpretations to every text. One very tall senior took me quite seriously. She wrote an essay about Meursault, from Camus' *The Stranger*, being autistic. It was a well-written and defended argument—if a little bit out there—and its fairly good score made an impression on me.

Besides the essays, I was also concerned about the surprisingly low scores my students received for their use of language. I queried IB about this and I received a paragraph response back suggesting that I was not as talented as I thought I was when it came to grammar and mechanics. I stopped asking questions after that.

When the scores for my class finally posted, everyone passed. Everyone. I was stunned. The principal was pleased. When I talked with the assistant principal about it, she gave me a terrific compliment. I told her that the students who earned 6's and 7's hadn't surprised me, but the students who had scored 4's and 5's were unexpected.

"That's teaching," she said.

This started a string of successful years when we received English score reports, one that continues to this day. Colleagues would start making noises about how the English

---

66 The head of school in London used to call England and the United States two countries separated by a common language. I think this is an example of what he meant. When we meet, ask me for my eggplant example. That was another example.

tests must be easier. Utter nonsense. We started with the end in mind—the three tests I described as well as the World Literature papers—and worked backwards to the ninth grade curriculum. We planned together, got the training we needed, and made the decision, as a group, that we cared about the results and that we thought our students could score well. And they did.

I am not suggesting it was easy. There were times when I was so tense I thought I would implode. A grizzled colleague would see me and say, "Remember, Charles, it's not Baghdad." It was good to be reminded.

***

There were a number of snow days that year, including one stretch of several days. For some reason, I remembered an opportunity I'd read about once, maybe in the back of a magazine called *Teacher*. I found the site for the National Endowment for the Humanities and, in a few snow days, applied for a summer institute on teaching Shakespeare. I was accepted. My summer would be spent at what my cohort came to call "Shakespeare Camp." I was going to Ashland, Oregon. And I was going to be paid for it.

Though I was told I was going to be picked up at the airport, I was still worried about finding the person who was supposed to pick me up. The flight landed, and I followed the signs for baggage claim. I prepared to turn the corner and have the building open out into the kind of airport craziness I was accustomed to in Baltimore or, to a greater extent, in Chicago. Instead, there was a kind of hallway, with a few baggage carousels and a young woman holding a card with my last name. That was it. As she drove me to campus, I asked her how to pronounce Oregon.

The Southern Oregon University dorm was not luxurious. I unpacked, oblivious to the container of Old Bay spice Kirsten had hidden in my suitcase to keep me from being homesick. After getting somewhat settled, I took the downhill walk to the center of the theater festival. I love the thrill of walking into a new theater or, in this case, a theater complex.

The days soon took on their shape. Some classroom time. Talks or free time at lunch. More Shakespeare-related activities in the afternoon. At night, we saw each of the Shakespeare plays twice—a treat that was made even more worthwhile because a few of the performers involved would have come to talk with us between our first show and the second. We also had the opportunity to see the other festival shows on our own. I fell in love with Nilo Cruz's work because of the production *Lorca in a Green Dress*, which I saw twice. I spent my entire stipend, if not more, in the festival's gift shop. Weekends meant doing the assigned reading or writing the assigned papers. They also meant whitewater rafting or a trip to a beautiful nearby lake. There was also a library of pretty much every Shakespeare and Shakespeare-related film, so we'd sometimes gather for a showing. And I soaked it all in, not only the Shakespeare, but everything my generally amazing group of colleagues shared with me. A few spent their whole summer, every summer, doing programs like the one in Ashland. I'm not sure I could do that, but there are tremendous opportunities out there. They shouldn't be so hard to find, and I wish more of them provided stipends rather than charging for participation, but they are out there.

***

I returned to school that fall, inspired by my experience and discouraged to find that I'd been assigned a desk in the English office and was going to be floating that year. I hate floating. I really hate floating.

And it wasn't just two rooms, either. And the rooms weren't close to each other; they were on separate floors. One room was filled with science tables. Another class met in at least three different locations because the ceiling kept caving in. I taught in the library for a short time. Kirsten bought me a pair of noise canceling headphones. I made sure everyone knew how unhappy I was and that I was not, despite my proximity to it, the keeper of the copier or someone to chat with while you waited for copies to be made.[67]

I started coaching during my second year in Baltimore. I was the junior varsity boys' basketball coach. The varsity coach was one of our deans. His assistant was a nice, knowledgeable fellow; I am not sure I ever learned his background. He didn't work at the school. I think coaches who don't otherwise work at the school are generally a mistake. They don't know the life of the school. Their priorities are their athletic

---

67 I am starting to realize that memory and memories are funny things. The contents of my memory have likely shifted during my flight. Please forgive me if I haven't gotten everything back into exactly the right place. I'm doing my best.

teams, something which some student-athletes don't need to experience. Much to the chagrin of our alumni, we were generally not a very good school when it came to athletics. We were also in a pretty competitive league, a league that included Dunbar, the one-time home of Mugsy Bogues, Sam Cassell, and Reggie Williams.

The head coach was all about motivation. His "coaching" consisted of telling his players over and over again that they lacked heart. His practices were pure scrimmages. I tried to be "one of the guys" who hung out in his office, but the conversations about expensive shoes and insider Baltimore talk tested my patience. I tried to be silent and supportive. But I am white. He is African-American. The principal was white. He, the head coach, was wary. It turned out he had a right to be.

We both struggled with our point guard. A decent ball handler (if mostly one-handed), he was argumentative and more concerned with winning practice drills than getting better. Years later, I would learn from Facebook that he'd had an argument with someone and been stabbed to death. He left behind four children.

I'm not sure I am going to get the sequence of these next two pieces right. Both pieces matter, but I don't think the sequence does. There were layoffs in the district. The head coach lost his dean position, but continued to coach. One night, though, I got an unusual call. It was the principal. It was the only time he ever called me at home. He was concerned that the head coach was stealing from the school. Perhaps this means that the call came after the layoff, that there was some kind of grudge theory at work. He asked me to write down the codes on the coach's keys, so he could see what he had access to, presumably so he could see if he had access to the spaces from which things had been stolen. I had no idea what had been taken, or that anything had been taken.

I was paralyzed by the call. Though my loyalty was definitely more with the principal than the coach, this seemed like crossing the line. I took a walk. I spoke with some friends about it, and I decided I couldn't do it. By the time I'd worked up the courage to tell the principal I couldn't do it, he acted like he'd forgotten the request.

Perhaps he had other things on his mind. I have always been somewhat and somewhat deliberately oblivious to school politics. I like to keep my head down, but even I recognized that something was amiss. The alumni was pushing hard to have the principal replaced. They longed, so I understood, for athletic glory, though that's probably a limited view. The principal was clearly on his way out. Even I, Captain Oblivious, figured this out. People from other schools came to interview him and various teachers about jobs for him at other schools. I didn't want him to leave, but I lacked the fortitude and knowledge to express myself. In short, even if I had summoned the courage, I didn't know where to turn to make my thoughts known. And I knew, or thought I knew, that I was in the minority. So I kept my mouth shut.

There were other departures, some forced, some voluntary. Having seen many people come and go from schools (including myself), I know there are reasons to decide how and when to reveal the information to colleagues and students. In general, I respect the wishes of the person leaving and how they choose to communicate their news. But one of the departing teachers had, in my mind, crossed a line. Without telling anyone of her impending departure, she committed to advising several students on a paper they had to write the following year. After I heard consecutive students declare that she was to be their advisor, I let my frustration get the best of me and made her departure known to them.

I know. I should have gone to her first and asked her how she thought this was going to work in a way that wouldn't end up putting more of a burden on those of us who were staying. But I didn't. And she wrote me a nasty note, which I deserved. For a few days, we both acted like middle schoolers. I freely admit that I started it. Maybe her actions irked me because I recognized them. No one wants to imagine themselves as replaceable. I've longed for messages from former students at former schools saying that my replacement did not live up to my standard; I've even gotten a few of those notes. But we are all replaceable. Every single one of us.

***

Bush: The Sequel had recently passed his alphabet soup of an educational quagmire, i.e., No Child Left Behind, and there was pressure on the administration to put some money behind it. Some bigwigs were looking for a show to take on the road to teach teachers. I applied and was accepted, probably less because of the brilliance of my proposal ("Reaching Reluctant Readers") than some combination of my department head's connections and the haste with which the team was put together.

There were seven cities on the tour, and most of them blur together in my memory. I remember my nervousness prior to my first presentation and the deep breath I took before reviewing my first set of evaluations.

The longer the summer went on, the less I enjoyed it. The government employees assigned to travel with us did little except for punch at their Blackberrys. It became increasingly apparent that the organizers had just hired their friends—some of whom were quite impressive—but left the rest of us feeling like outsiders. The Kansas Teacher of the Year, he of the museum within his classroom, commiserated with me about the arrangement.

The start of the next school year saw me stepping into two new roles: department head and young father. I had a small office and put up a sign, "It's the class sizes, stupid." The prior department head had left me a very thoughtful card in the desk, an extremely big pair of shoes to fill, and what she called her "middle drawer." Her middle drawer was the place where the bad ideas went not to die, but just to be neglected. Death by starvation. That's where I put all of the things that had come from our administration or from the school district that I knew I shouldn't throw out but I had no intention of making a high priority. The two biggest challenges, though, were two new people: a new English teacher and our new principal.

I had been part of hiring the new teacher. He'd seemed perfect. An alum of the school, he was a young African-American man with a background in English, social studies, and philosophy. From the very beginning, though, it became apparent that something just wasn't clicking. He had a first period African-American Literature class, and he was frequently running late, so I reluctantly offered to make copies for him each morning so he could be with his students.

He came to view that as his plan rather than an occasional favor. He was working on a graduate degree and seemed more intent on that than on his students. I can't remember all of the details about what went wrong, but it probably suffices to say that much of it was my fault, and, near the end, race and ambition got injected into the conversation. It ended poorly, to say the least.

Similarly, the new principal alienated just about everyone. His condescending speeches and general ineffectiveness left the school in turmoil. Administrative meetings filled with too many former English teachers who felt free to offer their input not based on their current job titles, but on mine. I went to a few administrative meetings outside the school until I found excuses not to.

Some faculty began to hear whispers in the wind that our principal was on his way out. Soon enough, the rumors turned out to be right. One day he was there and I was reading my first and only James Patterson novel on his recommendation, and the next day, he was gone. The school exhaled. The district brought in their polished fixer, a woman who would ask the male teachers to all wear ties and was proud of her PhD from the University of Phoenix.

By that time, Kirsten's job had soured, and she was being recruited elsewhere. Our daughter was less than a year old and did me the great favor of puking on a polyester school shirt the new principal had asked us all to wear on the same day. I didn't bother to stress about it. I was starting to say goodbye.

A colleague would later accuse me of reflecting on my years at City with rose-colored glasses. She was right. The school was, at this point, around 92 percent African-

American. I once overheard the following conversation:

A: *Want to know how to find the white students?*
B: *How?*
A: *Go to the IB classes.*

Not good. Something was indeed rotten in our state of Denmark.

It was clearly time to move on. St. Paul, Minnesota eventually proved to be the most attractive option for Kirsten. We spent yet another spring break looking for a house and arranging interviews for me. I started to follow the Minnesota Twins. We were on our way to the Land of 10,000 Lakes.

From Baltimore, I learned how much I relished being a part of a school with a history and being part of a department that pushed each other. I loved the challenge of the IB program and the world of literature it had made me find. I learned that people, including me, could be small. You would think that I'd learned that I was not made for administration. You'd be wrong.

Rant: A Bad Conversation with a Student

Perhaps it's of some comfort to you, but after twenty-five years, I still make mistakes. They may not be as aggressively stupid as they once were, but I still do things that make me kick myself.

I was using Nikki Giovanni's poem "Nikki-Rosa" in class recently as part of a continuing conversation about stereotypes. I thought the lesson was well put together. It had flowed nicely in the morning and in the first afternoon class. I incorporated a few literary terms—tone, connotation, etc.—and kept the emphasis on how it relates to the students' own creative writing. It's a good poem for students to imitate, and it allows me to gain some insights into who they are. Inevitably, a few students pop out who are really passionate about poetry and have drawerfuls of it that they want to show me. They tend to approach me after class: "I've got some poetry. Wanna see it? Wanna see it?" I fall for it every time. Such students give me hope.

In one class, though, I had several table groups who just would not stop talking. Our school's intervention specialist went over to one of them, and I'm honestly not sure whether she made the situation better or worse. And the quartet of girls were making very little progress. And when I walked by, one of the girls started to sing. That. Was. It.

I summoned her to the hall. Already a debatable move. I know it can embarrass students. I was so agitated that I didn't make myself slow down to think. And her reluctance to own the fact that she'd been talking non-stop and her defense of her singing ("You were asking about favorite poets. I was singing Tupac.") drove me over the edge.

We didn't talk. We bickered. Finally, I made a feeble effort to salvage an ending, a compromise, and I got the answer she knew I wanted, complete with the dismissive tone. I did take a breath before following her back into the classroom. Whatever face she showed her table crew made them laugh. I let it go, but it ate at me as I was stuck in traffic on the way home.

8
Harding High School
St. Paul, MN

When a friend learned that I'd be teaching in St. Paul, she recommended that I find the book *The Spirit Catches You and You Fall Down*, in order to learn more about the Hmong. I had to ask her to repeat that last word several times and then ask her to spell it. And then explain it.

With all of the required professional development involved in becoming part of the St. Paul Public Schools, in retrospect it's astonishing that there was absolutely nothing about the Hmong culture. I didn't learn not to be surprised when a student told me his weekend involved slaughtering a cow in his backyard. I didn't learn that Hmong students refuse all medical care. I didn't learn how to have a parent conference that involved a translator. As an English teacher, I didn't learn that the Hmong language did not have certain grammatical features that I took for granted, like verb tenses. Nor did I learn that there are only six Hmong last names.

My inexperience with Hmong last names led to an Abbott and Costello-ish first day of taking attendance. Sometimes, computer programs will cut off what are perceived to be middle names. I had a student on my roster who was, according to what I could tell, named Chu Cha. This was the conversation that ensued:

Me: Chu Cha?
Student: Who?

Me (thinking I might have been pronouncing it wrong): I think it says Chu Cha.

Student: Who?

Me: So maybe this person is not in this class?

Same student: I'm right here. My name is Chu Hu Cha.

Me: Oh.

When I got to the bottom of the roster and called "Mai Yang," three different girls raised their hands.

Then there were those students, both Hmong and otherwise, who would Americanize their names. I was never sure whether they were doing it because they were tired of hearing white people butcher them or were themselves in search of something more American to call themselves. It was another bit of cultural competency that I was sorely lacking.

This would be my second experience working at an IB school, but it would be quite a bit different than what I was used to. I looked at the book list I'd inherited and was concerned that *Their Eyes Were Watching God* would be too much to ask of ninth graders. I offered the book to the American Literature teachers. They were just short of incredulous. "You mean an IB teacher is sharing with us regular folks?" That was my first insight into departmental culture. This, I soon realized, left me with a book set comprised of only male writers, something I would not be able to remedy until the next school year.

The IB students did not follow a schedule that corresponded with the school bells. We had to rely on keeping an eye on the clock and sending our students down the hall at the appropriate time. It also meant that we were all teaching six sections of the same class, an exhausting assignment. As the day wore on, I could never remember what I had or had not explained to a particular group. And when an assignment came due, there went my weekend.

Since we all taught ninth grade, we were all part of the Ninth Grade Academy, an initiative sponsored by Bill Gates who, however well-intentioned he might be, continues to think that money entitles him to make educational policy.[68] The building had been undergoing renovations that previous spring when I'd interviewed. The changes, it turned out, were designed to support this Academy structure. But it seemed to me that no one really knew how to make these academies meaningful. Few teachers taught in just one academy, and few classes could be limited to students from just one academy. The ninth grade one was probably the purest example. It was also the most promising idea, since ninth grade was and remains such a pivotal year. Soon enough, though, the Gates funding ran out, and the Academy banners looked ridiculous. Where there was once at least effort to make the system meaningful, now there were barely superficial efforts.

Other things were new to me. We had a very active JROTC program, and I soon learned that every school in the district did. It was easy to get over my bias against such programs once I got to know the leaders involved. Whatever I thought of (and think of) military recruitment and preparation happening in schools (especially schools with large minority populations like ours), these were good people, interested in teaching well and supporting the "regular" teachers.

One of my sharpest English students was in the JROTC program. She was a good writer with a sly sense

---

68 See also our current Secretary of Education.

of humor. She had a strong sense of self-discipline that the JROTC program only enhanced. We got along well—until one day we didn't. She was in the last of my six sections and her shockingly out-of-character behavior combined with my end-of-day fatigue exhausted my patience. I told her she was staying after school.

By then, I'd calmed down somewhat. Or maybe it was because I thought I knew her well and that her behavior was so out of character that I approached the conversation from that angle. I told her I thought that when a student's behavior was so jarringly and unexpectedly different, it usually meant that something else was going on. I turned out I was right. She was having thoughts of suicide and starting to formulate a plan. Her behavior was a signal; she wanted my help.

One way I learn about my students is to ask them to write me a letter of introduction.[69] And, since I am an English teacher, I ask them what they like to read. This one name came up over and over again. Now I'm pretty well-read, but I'd never heard of this author before. So I went straight from school to the bookstore. I had to know who this author was who had so captivated my students. I searched alphabetically. Nothing. Finally, I found a salesperson and told him my story.

Salesperson: So what's the author's name?

Me (consulting my notes): Manga

Salesperson (imagine a face reflecting the fact that he's encountered the stupidest person in the world)

Me (checking my notes again): Yep. (Still thinking that

---

69 I have since changed to asking them to tell me their story. It yields better, more insightful writing rather than the scattered lists that the letter assignment often produced.

the salesperson was the idiot.) Manga. M-a-n-g-a.

(Salesperson indicates that I should follow, and he leads me to the manga section of the bookstore. He leaves me to it and goes to laugh about me to all of the other employees at the bookstore, the people who ran the pet store, a few of the dogs and guinea pigs at that pet store, and so on.)

Another gap in my cultural competency.

Thus was my introduction to manga. In fact, I'm pretty sure I hadn't even read a graphic novel to that point, so I had the students introduce me to manga and how to read it. I soon gained enough of an understanding to ask the students to create a manga version of one of the episodes in *The Odyssey*. For the most part, their efforts were spectacular.

Though it's been some years since then, I still haven't read much beyond the classic teachable graphic novels. I would come to *Persepolis* first because the news flew around our department that, at the urging of a staff member, the principal had confiscated the students' copies of *Persepolis* in the middle of class. Given my passionate interest in protecting students' right to read and particularly appalled at the lack of process involved in the decision, I read it quickly and was part of the successful effort to get the books back in students' hands.

Graphic novels have one serious obstacle to confront before they can become more commonly used in the classroom: They are simply too expensive. I wanted to teach *Persepolis* one year, but I had to cut it to stay within my book budget. While I don't suggest that the graphic novel versions of books replace studying the books themselves, they can be a useful supplement or an option for differentiation.

Beyond the new literary horizons my students

were opening up for me, my time at Harding followed a predictable path. One of the patterns I'd noticed by now is that my happiness at a school is somewhat dependent on the principal. I didn't care for the one we had. He was a lower school transplant, quite invested in the jargon of the day (i.e., "Professional Learning Communities," or PLCs). As with a great many initiatives, this one was introduced with much style and little substance. The staff-wide cynicism just deepened.

I also continued my pattern of finding field trips. A local theater was showing *Romeo and Juliet*. I remember the production as being average, but the energy of the theater's education director after the show was memorable. She came running to catch us before we boarded the buses. Someone from our section, she was certain, had thrown a condom on stage during the scene when Romeo stays with Juliet overnight. Publicly, I was appalled and tried to discover the culprit.[70] Privately, I was a little bit proud of whoever it was for knowing what was going on during that scene. Incidents like this did not diminish my passion for field trips in the slightest. If we want students to learn how to be at a show or a museum, they have to practice.

When the year finally settled down a bit, I decided to attack the files that my predecessor had left behind. I was in the first or second day of this purge when my department head entered and told me that the twelfth grade IB teacher

---

70 No luck. The theater gave students tickets to try to make them feel like it was a genuine theater experience. There were real volunteer ushers and programs as well. They wanted you to write down which student was in which seat. That was just not going to happen.

was retiring and asked whether I wanted that class. I stopped sorting the files.

But the course of true class assignments never does run smooth. The department was up in arms. There had been no process for deciding who got to teach the class. Anyone, many of them reasoned, could teach the class, and almost everyone had been there longer than me. Why did I *deserve* it? Therein lies the rub[71] found frequently in schools. The "higher" level courses are assumed to be easier because, the stereotype goes, student behavior is better. Class assignments, some argue, should be based on seniority. I sat through the inevitable meeting and in a rare show of good judgment kept my mouth shut. I got the class. The department got its process. Or at least had its complaints heard.

One of my first goals when I assumed the class was to change the culture, particularly around testing. I made it clear from day one that everyone would test and that everyone could succeed. It was a long slog to get everyone registered. One parent held out. Their younger son, whom I'd taught as a ninth grader, was the smart one, they insisted. He would test; he would succeed. The older one, well, they didn't want him to be disappointed. I persisted. The deadline for registration was on a Monday. I told the student on the Friday before that that I thought he wanted to test and that his job over the weekend was to convince his parents. He came in on Monday with a signed registration form. When I saw his still skeptical mother later, I said (half) jokingly that if he passed, then she owed me cake.

---

71 Too much?

It turned out that she made a pretty good carrot cake.

After that first year with the twelfth grade class, the news of changes started to spread throughout the school. The principal was leaving. The Department Head who had interrupted my filing was retiring. His co-department head was taking a Fulbright year in Prague. The department looked to me to lead, and again I fell for it.

In addition to welcoming the teacher from Prague, I soon had a much more serious challenge. One of our best teachers became very ill. We needed a replacement and we needed one soon. I helped find one, but she turned out to be terrible. Ultimately, the new principal used his executive power and hired an old friend who turned out to be OK.

I took on a student teacher during my third year at Harding. In Nashville, since I was something of a known quantity because Kirsten was at the School of Education at Vanderbilt, I got some of their more challenging teachers. This time, though, I got lucky. This student teacher was a natural. She took over the classes with few problems. Her biggest challenge was that she was doing her student teaching at the same time as she was preparing to get married.

Between my leadership duties and my student teacher program, I wasn't teaching a full load. The job, quite frankly, wasn't inspiring me. And we had a new son. I could feel my feet getting itchy. That's when Kirsten sent me a job posting.

The Blake School, a private school I knew little about, was looking for a PK-12 Language Arts department chair. I read the description carefully and when I saw it included teaching responsibilities, I decided to try for it. I had moved into leadership positions at three consecutive schools. It was time, I thought, to see if I could start in a leadership position. It was time, I thought, to see if that's where I fit.

I went in for what turned out to be the first of a three-day interview process. The Blake School has three different campuses in three different cities. One of the secretaries was kind enough to MapQuest all of the directions for me, but I still got lost going to one half of the lower school which was located in a far suburb. When I finally pulled over to call the cell phone number I was given in case I had trouble, I was told I had gone one Target store too far.

When I finally made it to the school, I had to gather myself. I was in the middle of a conversation with the assistant principal when two girls came bounding up to her, their minds so full of energy and ideas that they couldn't be contained by normal walking. The assistant principal turned, put her hands on her thighs and responded to their excitement in just the way I'd want someone to respond to my own children. I was hooked.

"It reminds me," I told tell Kirsten when I called her on a break, "of Georgetown Day." She knew that meant I wanted the job.

A few pieces stand out from the interview. The Middle School assistant principal who saw me dragging and offered me caffeine. The conversation in the Lower School staff room bordered on aggressive, a tone that would foreshadow my work there. The Upper School division director arrived late (also soon to be a regular theme), and he argued with the Science Department head about curriculum mapping. Conversations with the head of school about, among other things, the performance-based pay system the school was, at his urging, beginning the following year.

The person who was running the interview process was the person I would end up reporting to. When the epic interview was over, she gave me a date and said that if I hadn't heard anything by then, they had decided not to pursue my candidacy.

I didn't hear anything by the date she mentioned. Or the next day. I wrote her a note thanking her for the opportunity to interview and asking to be kept in mind if the position opened again in the future. Before the note reached her,[72] she called to offer me the job. After a brief negotiation, I accepted.

Since I don't like these things to leak through the inevitable grapevine, I informed my department and administration immediately. My principal made the best argument against my departure.

"They don't need you," he said.

"Well, I don't want to work with you," I thought.[73] So I left.

Harding taught me a lot about expectations. A student complained at one point, "You're asking too much of us; we're Harding students." I think that comment was indicative of how everyone—students, staff, parents— saw themselves. Consider the mother who didn't want her son to take his IB test. Consider, also, the teacher who claimed at a meeting that the way to get more black male students to read was to give them magazines. I was furious. I said that I could get any student to read *Hamlet*. When the facilitator asked me how, I

---

72   The old-fashioned way, with a stamp and everything.

73   Maybe there is something to this whole maturity theory.

sputtered. I could only manage, "Because that's my job."

There were also my own expectations, expectations I formed before making myself more aware of the population I was serving. One book didn't make me culturally competent. I am still in touch with several of my former Harding colleagues, and most of them are still there. The place inspired that kind of loyalty, just not in me. I had once planned a life that involved spending my career at one school. I guess I'd been trying to make God laugh.

Rant: The Follow-Up

Remember that student with whom I had the bad conversation in the last rant? She was absent for the next two days, a pattern of hers that was, I learned, far from out of character. Still, I made myself the center of the world for a bit and thought maybe she'd taken the days off because she was frustrated with me. Two calls to her mother only got me as far as an answering machine.

After being out Thursday and Friday, she returned on Monday. Having previously arranged it with her third period teacher, I asked her to step out of class and join me in the principal's office. We have no other spaces for these kinds of conversations. I did my best to muster my "I" statements and present things in a far different way than I had the previous week, but her reaction was mostly one of confusion. At most, she thought I was making too much of our exchange. Part of me wondered whether she was posing. She did participate, but her comments were generally short. When I seemed unable to communicate effectively, the principal, a great if at times long-winded communicator, stepped in, and his comments seemed to alleviate some of the confusion. We found a place to resolve it, or maybe it was just a place to stop. The principal and I debriefed afterwards, and his suggestion was that when such conversations fall flat that it's best to just let them be. In essence, I should act like the conversation hadn't happened.

Her conduct was better that afternoon. I think what I learned that day and the subsequent day is that she has a hard time staying with an activity for a sustained period of time. When her patience or concentration runs out, the behaviors emerge. She's far from the only ninth grader with that issue. It wouldn't be a bad thing for me to try to break up the class into shorter sections. Perhaps by withdrawing my focus on her conduct, I was able to see something I could work on.

Several months later, this student now says I'm her favorite teacher and consistently asks to stay for an extra period because she doesn't like the class after mine. Now if I could only get her to do her work more often.

9
The Blake School of Excellence
Minneapolis, MN

It is difficult to write about my experience at Blake for three reasons. First, my experience there was so multilayered and tangled that it doesn't easily fit a coherent narrative. Second, it ended with me being asked to resign, the new niceness that fools absolutely no one, including the subsequent employer. Third, it was a disaster for our children. Where to begin?

The problem started even before my tenure officially began. The Upper School division director, known for both his meticulousness and his lateness,[74] called to suggest my teaching schedule. A part-time middle school teacher was expected to go on maternity leave shortly after the year started. I could take her classes in the middle school and one AP English[75] class (eleventh grade) in the high school. Keep in mind that these two schools are *in different cities*. I should have said no. I should have said that this was not setting me up for success. But I didn't. I said fine.

---

74 Two of my favorite quotations from him: "I like schedules because they don't talk back" and "English teachers are a dime a dozen."

75 The department had tried to outsmart the school's administration (as it would many times while I was there) by undermining efforts at tracking via AP by making *all* eleventh graders take AP Language and Literature. While I recognize the spirit of this mini-rebellion, it was a move based on the principles of the department not on what was best for the students. I tried and failed to undo it. I understand that it has since been undone.

I spent the summer making myself familiar with the reading list and meeting as many people as I could. The summer reading list for the incoming eighth graders (the class I would be teaching for a while) was, curiously, all Holocaust literature. When I asked about the selection of *The Merchant of Venice* for World Literature in ninth grade, I was told it was the Jewish book for the World Literature class.[76]

I still remember the first day of teaching my eleventh graders. Ever since a student in Baltimore had answered my opening day favorite movie question by asking (sincerely), "What if my favorite movie is a porno?" I had abandoned that question. I'm not sure if I asked a special question that day, but I must have asked the students how they spent their summers. One student said he had been at a wakeboarding camp. I took a breath. I didn't even know such things existed. I was in a whole new world.

The middle school teacher went on maternity leave in the second week of September. I finished the unit we'd she'd started and moved into *Romeo and Juliet*, a book I love to teach. I may have stretched it out too long. I made a pretty good connection with that grade, trying to build relationships with students I'd be working with for years. I didn't know at that time that my tenure would end before they graduated high school.

The two basic instructions I was given that first year were to form relationships and to learn the curriculum. Unbeknownst to me, it had been decided that I did not need to concern myself too much with the Lower School my

---

76 I did manage to have it dropped.

first year. I wish someone had told me that. The principal made her displeasure at my first year performance known to my supervisor and said nary a word to me. This triangular communication, a regular feature of Blake, always reminded me of the way middle schoolers conducted their first romantic relationships.

The thing about having to work in four buildings in three cities was that those of us who held the PK-12 positions were always in a hurry. My car, just as gas prices were flirting with the $4-per-gallon mark, became my office. It also became my lunch room. I was always in a hurry, and when you combine the tone I can sometimes seem to have as well as my sense of needing to be in a hurry, I believe I dug myself a relationship hole from the very beginning, one I'd always be trying to repair, not without some successes, but never completely successfully.

Something else set me back, too: my Jewishness. Have you ever been to Minnesota? There is a concept called Minnesota Nice that is not anywhere near as positive as it sounds. It means people will be welcoming and friendly, but if you can't cite which Minnesota high school you attended, the friendliness will only go so far. We found this to be true in our personal lives as well. When I was at Blake, there were, as far as I knew, five of us who were Jews. While the school, which counts Al Franken as an alum, had a Jewish student population,[77] there wasn't much of one among the faculty. This lack of diversity was not unknown to the administration.

---

77 Admitted, some (including Franken) claim, to increase the school's academic standing and reputation.

The school was in the midst of a series of diversity training seminars. We had a visiting professor leading us, and she could definitely rub people the wrong way. (Perhaps it was all of the references to "Super Whitey.")

When it comes to teaching English or Language Arts (itself a debate), the easy place to focus on diversity is on author selection, and that's what we did. We focused on finding books that were age-appropriate, that featured a similar number of male and female protagonists, and were written by a balance of male and female authors who are from different times and places in the world.

As important as it was to discuss what books we were going to teach (a patronizing book about the fur trade that was used in the fourth grade took an epic amount of time to address), I knew there had to be more to diversity than that. It was time to move past what we taught to how we taught. Still, I struggled. When a female teacher of color said she had to teach her students how to be white before she could teach them literature, I recoiled. I wondered about all of the time spent on characters who are not obviously present (black men) in Tim O'Brien's *The Things They Carried*. As with most things during my time at Blake, I think we made some progress. There were some incremental changes, but those took a lot of time and a lot of meetings. I tried to guide us to how we gave feedback, but could never gain much traction there. And I am quite sure that I alienated more than a few people along the way.

More contentious than the diversity issue, though, was the new performance-based pay structure. Perhaps because I flatter myself that I would earn it, I have always been intrigued by the idea. The way the head of school explained it to me made sense. After approximately a dozen or so years at the school, he had decided to spend some of his political capital on making this work. A couple of things had already complicated the landmine that is merit pay.

The staff, in a non-binding referendum, had voted pretty strongly against the institution of the program. When the administration decided to proceed anyway, the faculty seemed confused by the concept of "non-binding." And there'd already been a compromise. Instead of an all-or-nothing system, there were going to be three tiers of performance-based pay. That did nothing to make the policy simpler or more palatable. And then a board member apparently said at a staff-wide meeting that everyone was a wonderful teacher, or something like that. It was before my time, but the story had legs.

So, a bad teaching schedule, being first in a new administrative role, tense diversity training, and the divisive concept of performance-based pay— that was a lot to confront all at once. I should have seen the writing on the wall right then and there.

***

There was so much going on in my time at Blake that it's difficult to communicate the dysfunction I encountered. It's easier to understand when you look at the evolution of a program's problems over time, though, and none stands out in my mind more than History Day.

History Day,[78] founded in 1974, was designed as a competition. By the time I arrived at Blake, the ninth grade team, consisting of both World Literature and World History teachers, had largely (but not completely) abandoned the competitive elements. They also had decided that they could improve upon the project. I heard grumblings from all corners that the project, which pretty much consumed an entire quarter of the ninth grade year, needed to go. There were high school teachers who flatly refused to teach ninth grade because they couldn't stand the project. I had to learn more about it.

After four years of experiencing it (which includes one year of teaching it), I can't say with any confidence or concision exactly what the History Day assignment really was. Students were supposed to find and propose some element of an historical incident—the IRA's battles with England, for example—then research their piece of history and write an extended paper. Next, they were to convert what they'd learned into a ten-minute play focused on the non-dominant narrative of that particular piece of history.

Got it? Yeah, me neither.

Every year, the group, its own kind of private cluster of self-appointed guardians of morality, would add another page of instructions, thinking that with just a bit more clarity, with just a few more instructions, the project would finally be clear. What they never realized is there was no making the thing better; it was broken from within.

During the first year, I just watched from afar and asked

---

78 nhd.org

to be invited to the final performances. I watched a handful of plays that year and saw a mellow and completely wonderful teacher appear stressed out for the first and only time in my years with him. I could only manage to stay for two or three plays at a sitting. They all had one basic problem; they were boring.

In my second year, I tried a different strategy. I asked to follow a few pairs of students as they made their way through the process. This was of particular interest because the ninth grade class included a lot of the eighth grade students I'd taught the year before. I expressed my concern to one particularly unqualified teacher who had kind of backed her way into a teaching position. She'd started or help start a summer outreach program that was and is justifiably a point of pride for the school. She had no real qualifications to teach, however, so whenever a discussion of actual history came up, she was, quite knowingly and self-consciously, lost. I wondered about the chances for success of one particular pair who I'd taught the year before. I received a long email in return about how the students were, in fact, having to practice all sorts of writing skills. She did not mention two things. They were being asked to practice them *all at the same time* and *at the same time as they were trying to teach themselves about Gandhi's Salt March or whatever their chosen topic was.* One of the two students withdrew from the school in the middle of the project. I don't know if there was a direct connection.

For my fourth year, I assigned myself to ninth grade. I thought that if I went through the project myself then I could gain more credibility with the team, a team whose smugness was increasing in proportion to the scrutiny of their brainchild. I attended the weekly self-affirmation sessions (called "Team Meetings") and sought to understand and implement the curriculum the best we could. It was no use. I was hopeless and befuddled. And the plays were boring too.

After stressful meeting upon stressful meeting, the Upper School division director, who pretty much bailed on offering any support for me, pulled the plug on History Day. No one believed the claim that the project was just going on hiatus. I received a half dozen whispered thank yous as word filtered through the Blakevine, the unofficial path for the school's gossip. I was ready to move on, to reset things. I proposed a calendar of funded professional days to re-work the curriculum. My name was removed from the email, which was then circulated with, I was told, disparaging remarks about me. I had tried to phrase it as an opportunity to share resources, to suggest that over the years, as the team had shifted, different elements had been introduced, revised, etc., and it would be great to get everything in one place, so each team could have its choice of units. Still, it was probably too late for me to do anything but be the hatchet man.

In the end, we were given one afternoon to redefine the program. One of my department members, more loyal to the team than to any notion of what was good for students, pretty much proposed the same History Day project by another name. She was a binder teacher. That is to say, once she had things figured out, then that was it. She was going back to the same binder year after year. I told her, in no uncertain terms, that we were not going to replace History Day with a facsimile of it. The whole curriculum, from the use of *The Merchant of Venice* in my first year to the coloring book assignment, needed to be reconsidered.

I laid out a plan for reviewing the curriculum, but the new head of school announced, without consulting me, that we'd follow a procedure she'd used before. I asked for a meeting with her about that, and she said she'd be glad to come talk with the department about it, that she would face it "head on." She then showed up and the department lost the courage of its convictions and we talked about pretty much nothing. She did, again without consulting me, give the department permission to order whatever books they wanted whenever they wanted. She undid four years of my efforts at streamlining[79] the process with one flippant comment. We never did figure out how to replace History Day much less reconsider the curriculum—at least during what remained of my tenure at Blake.

***

Though I am skeptical of education books that have numbers in the title (are there really only five dysfunctions of a team?), my philosophy of department leadership consists of three parts:

1. Get the right people.
2. Get them what they need.
3. Get out of the way.

When I started at Blake, it didn't take long for three teachers to jump out at me as not being the right people—two

---

79 I did more than just streamline it, but that's enough of a comment for now.

in the middle school and one in the high school. I decided that the best way to make my mark would be to deal with these three quickly.

The teacher in the high school already had already received coaching from an outside consultant who had, in a self-fulfilling prophecy, determined that the coaching had worked and that the teacher was fixed. When I later queried this consultant, it turned out that she had never taught in high school and did not have any background in secondary education.

I sat in on this teacher's class a lot. Too much, he complained. It was too much pressure. Word quickly got around that the spotlight was on him. One colleague told me that if I was part of the reason that he was not invited back to the school for the following year, I would do irreparable damage to my credibility with the department. Others told me there was no way they would allow their own children to be in his class. It was a difficult way to begin my work at the school.

The two teachers at the middle school were in starkly different situations. One was part-time, and[80] after just a few visits to her classroom it became apparent that she was the type of teacher who thought just showing up was enough. There was no preparation and only a little effort to make good use of class time. She'd read a little from the current book, comment on it, take a few comments, ask about some vocabulary words, and then move on. She was highly resistant to any coaching, and she was toxic in meetings

---

80 I had been asked to consider the number of teachers in my department who were part-time and whether I thought it was a good idea. Full disclosure: most of them were female. The males who taught part-time had other jobs at the school, like being deans. This, too, was not easy to navigate.

and in the hallways—forever complaining, gossiping, and trying to poison the relationships between the faculty and administration. Rather than fire her outright, though, we shifted around the staffing situation to offer her a role we knew she didn't want. It felt dirty. Manipulative. It was, I learned, a common technique at Blake. But it had the desired effect: She was gone.

The other middle school teacher was the one Jewish teacher I mentioned earlier. On the plus side, he was a good person to have in a middle school. He was a compassionate advisor. He taught both English and social studies, which made him economically efficient. The problem, though, was that he wasn't very good at either.

He had his shtick, and it all centered on him. And it was the same shtick every year. His willingness to be coached was something akin to the turtle in the well problem or a Bruce Springsteen song—one step up and two steps back. He, too, was more than a little toxic in the halls, forever railing against the endless injustices "they" were doing to him.

His sense of entitlement was astounding. I was told that he'd received a great deal of money from the school to pursue (expensive) opportunities that were only tangentially related to teaching—a conference on storytelling in Italy, for example. We also had a budget for a writer-in-residence in the middle school, and he saw it not as an opportunity to work with someone or even learn from someone but as a break for himself. "It's good for the students to work with someone different," he'd say as he sat at his desk grading the endless piles of busywork he'd assigned.

He saw questions as threatening. When I asked him how his vocabulary skits helped students learn the words, he was astounded that I'd question him. He, and he was not alone here, would claim that things "worked"[81] because he said they worked, and I should leave him alone because we were supposed to be an Independent school, not an independent school. To him, Independent meant he could do whatever he wanted whenever he wanted. To those of us charged with running the school, it did mean that we could allow teachers freedom to innovate; mostly, though, it meant we were independent of the state's requirements. We did not have to attend to the Common Core, for example, or the same testing requirements.

By the time I took the job, this teacher had already been on what we called "assessment" once. That was, at least in theory, our way of warning a teacher that his next contract may not be offered. He was again placed on assessment while I was there. After I left, he was placed on assessment again. When is enough enough? He survives still, as far as I know. I thought it was hard to get rid of someone at a public school. I didn't expect it to be so difficult at a private school.

The other part of making sure we had the right personnel was hiring. I would get box loads of resumes delivered from the head of school's office whenever there was an opening. They generally fell into a few categories:

1. People trying and failing to get tenure at a college

2. Writers who needed to make some money while they were writing

---

81 Whatever that meant.

3. People with one-year of experience here, there, and everywhere

4. Teachers

I scoured the resumes for indications that the candidate might be a person of color. Professional organizations were usually a good source of clues. As far as I knew, every private school was seeking more teachers of color. And the teachers of color that I knew at Blake knew it. One (other) middle school teacher openly said that his skin color made him invincible.

I spent a lot of time on this process. I likened the prospect of hiring someone for a permanent position to appointing someone to the Supreme Court. Generally, people didn't want to leave Blake. I wanted, I tried to explain to anyone who protested the parade of candidate lunches, interviews, and demo lessons, to get it as right as I could. Now that I think of it, my batting average was not very good.

The first big whiff came when the high school teacher I mentioned above, the one who thought I was sitting in on his class too often, decided for personal reasons at pretty much the last minute that he needed a leave. By the time I was brought into the situation, we had two candidates. One, I'd met. She fell into the struggling writer category and had a few personal attributes I didn't admire. I arranged to meet the other at a nearby coffee shop. She'd already received an enthusiastic reception from others, and I was impressed as well. But when we hired her, she proved to be a disaster. She had no sense of how to plan, no ability to build rapport with students, no passion for the job. She was utterly lost in front of the classroom. What was absolutely exasperating was at the good-bye luncheon I was pushed to arrange for her, she was as engaging as she'd been during the interview process. This time, though, I had it figured out. She was great . . . with adults.

More big misses followed. There was the fill-in teacher who flirted with students. There was the volatile teacher whose candidacy had been pushed by the then-assistant head of school. There was the excellent interim person whose candidacy I backed, but recommended someone else because that was the consensus of the department. Very fortunately, I was overruled there, though the person I had initially recommended was hired in another department and became a mess.

I even failed in my diversity initiatives. During a search for a new middle school teacher, we had narrowed the field down to two candidates. The first really impressed me in the interview, but there was one problem. She was a suburban white woman, and we already had plenty of those. Our other main candidate was quirky. We'd flown him in from the Seattle area after he was recommended by a faculty member and interviewed well. He was a male candidate of color. He made rap YouTube videos about everything from grammar to Shakespeare. He would be an unconventional choice, and I wanted him. It was time to go past lip service about diversity at the school and to take a chance. Over the objections of the department, I recommended him and the head of school offered him the job. He turned it down. I never found out why. We offered it to the other candidate, and she has been amazing. The only thing that makes me wince is to look at pictures of her with her team of teachers—all white, suburban women.

Then there's the one I thought I did right. She had private school experience and actually seemed to want to be a teacher. She had Minnesota roots so would likely stay if we chose her. It took fewer than ten minutes of her model lesson for me to send an email to the other person watching the lesson. "This could work," I wrote. And I worked hard to get her there. To her credit, she dove in. She took over the newspaper and got it humming. She was our first full-time female teacher. She was teaching in the upper grades. Up until that point, we'd had neither. She was enthusiastic, had content knowledge, wanted to put her sons in the school, had a hockey coaching[82] husband who was trying to find a role at the school—all signs, to paraphrase the Magic 8 Ball, were pointing to her as a good hire. And mostly, she was.

She did, however, turn out to be something of a gossip and a toxic presence. The head of school had told me that when you hire someone, they become loyal to you. She apparently missed that memo as she took more than a few potshots at me (while lamenting the indirect communication inherent in "Minnesota Nice") without talking with me first. And while she was often strong when it came to individual books (though she more than regularly was just winging it), her thought process had little coherence to it. She confused curriculum with meaning the march of one book after another. She was not prone to self-reflection or incorporating feedback. She was the show. I am sure she's largely doing fine now, though—still mistaking energy and enthusiasm for

---

82 The reverence for hockey in Minnesota and at Blake has to be endured to be believed.

effectiveness, still sure of her own particular brand of genius.

***

Despite the missteps and backbiting, I really did love the work. It was challenging, exciting, hard, and often lonely. The part I did not love, however, was the bureaucracy. There were *so many* meetings at Blake. There were meetings in all sorts of shapes and sizes, each with their own name, but often with overlapping agendas. One year, one of these meetings was consumed (for consecutive weeks) by how to accommodate the traditional semester end projects into the exam schedule because no one could possibly give up or modify what they'd always done. So we reviewed draft after draft after draft of the exam schedule, each on its own color of paper. I think I tuned out after goldenrod.

We met as AA, MSAC, USAC, and LSAC. We met as department chairs, we met with our departments (Lower, Middle, Upper) and, six times a year, we met with the Lower, Middle and Upper School departments together. We met with our supervisor two, if not three times a month, and we met to discuss hiring and any other issues or projects that arose. If we were not in a meeting, we were preparing for the next one. And many of the meetings had the same, if not overlapping agendas. And some clearly had no agendas at all and instead became opportunities for, in one example, the Upper School division director to complain, essentially, about doing her job.

I had been told in the past and received the same feedback in my early years at Blake that I lacked the requisite poker face at meetings, so I adopted the Harkness discussion leader move of avoiding eye contact. Then I was told that I seemed asleep. Finally, I was told that I never hung around for the post-meeting conversations. When I suggested that we might spend some time coaching meeting leaders on how to use the time effectively so that there was no need for these informal post-meeting chats, there was no argument with my message, just my tone.

The PK-12 meetings were the most common source of complaint. Try as I might, I found it incredibly difficult to develop an agenda that would be useful for a PK teacher trying to teach a student how to hold a pen *and* an eleventh grade teacher trying to help a student write a college essay. I had a few successful meetings and pieces of meetings. In my last two years, I scheduled one meeting off-site, first at a nearby art gallery and then, inspired by the book *Shop Class as Soulcraft*, in our own shop classroom. But I canceled the final one of my final year. I just couldn't muster up the energy or ideas.

I know it is a cliche to complain about meetings, but think about your staff or department meetings. How many of them have been useful? Inspiring? Contained elements that could not be communicated in an email? To their credit, my current administration runs very tight and focused meetings. Mostly, though, I think we schedule meetings to justify ourselves. This is what we think we need to do. We pretend we are seeking buy-in or genuine input, but we're not. If there is a good book about meetings, I didn't find it. I mean, I adopted the "start on time, end on time" approach. I adopted the "inform, discuss, decide" trifecta. I tried starting meetings with a poem. I tried ending meetings with a poem. I tried delegating. I made myself the note taker to try to make sure others had a voice. Whatever meeting magic exists in the universe, I, at best, only found it randomly and occasionally.

Even now, I wince at the prospect of a meeting. I avoid them when I can, especially at the district level. When I'm at one, I try to avoid bringing my computer because I know it will distract me. I don't set out trying to be disrespectful. I was known, for a time, for writing epic letters during meetings. Sometimes, I take elaborate visual notes. I try to avoid excessive snacking, but generally fail. The worst, though, is when meetings deteriorate into sessions of complaining, and nowhere was that more frequent, in my experience, than at Blake. The faculty with the least grounds for complaint definitely complained the most.

To be fair, the American School in London probably had more money and more complaining than Blake. And more meetings. Perhaps there's a correlation? I think since I entered Blake as an administrator who teaches, the complaining hit me harder. And it all started with a roast.

I can't remember whether it was Back to School Night or Open House Night or some other event. But every year, we would go downstairs to the already amazing cafeteria[83] and there would be white tablecloths, fancy place settings, and one of the chefs would be behind a table ready to carve a roast for all of us to enjoy. Now, of course, everyone knew his name, because we were the type of people who prided

---

83 No kidding. During my interview, I had lunch at the middle school. The soup that day? Vichyssoise. And yes, I had to look up how to spell that.

ourselves on knowing the names of custodians, chefs, security guards, etc.

And this is not only what people got and what they expected, it's what they thought they deserved. The people who talked most loudly and proudly about how we had to teach the students about their privilege tended to be the most privileged ones of all. Want a part-time job to fit in with your life? Sure. Want to cap your classes at sixteen because any more than that will cause you to throw a diva-sized temper tantrum? Not a problem. Think you're entitled to a job just because you're you? Because you've decided that you have some kind of monopoly on virtuousness? OK, dokey. Want to spend a great deal of the school's money on a whim because you think it's the right thing to do? Here's the checkbook. Want to criticize me for sharing information because when you do it it's called "transparency"? Have at it. Want to turn in forms late, show up late, ignore instructions and more without consequences because that's what makes for an independent school? Go crazy. Want to complain incessantly about not having enough time to talk with other teachers and then spend the time you're given whining? Sure. Want to ignore research because you know better and to suggest otherwise amounts to a personal affront worthy of complaining to someone else about? Stand in line. Interested in lamenting how much time it takes you to grade papers but refuse to take any feedback about the papers you assign or how you grade them? Join the club. Have to fill out an application to get the school to pay for you to go on a trip to Africa rather than just saying you're interested? A box of Kleenex for you. Pretty sure you are doing the perfect job and can't possibly take input or do anything more because you can't manage the stress of it all and will therefore need to spend more time at your cabin or on your boat? I know where you can work.

I guess I'm still a little bitter.

***

So, after all this, what finally wrote my fate? I think it probably started with email.

At Blake, I got swallowed by email. First of all, I was on every single mailing list at the school. My inbox grew exponentially. And since I was rarely in the same zip code as the person I wanted to talk to, I grew to rely on it.

I admit, it was easier than talking with people, a situation I shy away from even in my personal life. When I take the Meyers-Briggs test, I am always an "I," for Introverted. (I am always a "J" for Judgemental too, but you probably figured that out already.) Too often I would email someone in the same building rather than going to their office or classroom to have the conversation in person.

Email tone is a tricky thing. I mean, first, there is the amount. I like specific emails that come with specific subject lines. That makes them easier to track. My colleagues and direct reports were less fond of this approach. So I tried to consolidate. Then there was the question of which me was writing. Was I writing as a teacher or as their supervisor? I relayed one story about someone at another school in my position who would wear one color tie when he was a peer and another as a supervisor. I wasn't going to do that. But I did consider different fonts.

Then there's the word choice. I was never an emoji user, but I soon learned that I had little idea of the impact of my words and phrases, especially when I was in a rush. And I was generally always in a rush, both because of the nature of the position and because our children were young at the time. I had to get them from day care by a certain time and wanted to spend time with them before their then very short days ended.[84]

Despite our repeated instructions not to surprise our teachers with their end-of-year evaluations, I was pummeled each June by the feedback I received. At the end of my fourth year at Blake, as the person who had hired me was leaving and the person who was taking her place was stepping into the role, I saw the beginning of my end.

The truth is, as upsetting as the prospect was, time had added another layer of frustration to my experience with the school, one that made me recollect a common theme in my initial three-day interview. I'd asked the faculty members who also had children at the school what that experience was like. While I didn't keep statistics, I walked away with the impression that most responses had been something akin to, "It it perfect for X; it did not work out for Y." And that's what was happening with us. Our daughter, the older child, was being served fairly well by the school. She had started to notice some class issues, which were going to come up at some point, but for the most part she seemed to be flourishing. Our son, on the other hand, was not. And while we never expected it to be a perfect match, we did expect the school to do more to meet his needs. At the time, I put its failure

---

84 Now at least one stays up later than me.

to do so down to flaws I ascribed to individual members of the staff. While I still think that was partially responsible, I think it was, to a great extent, a system error. Rather than having the fortitude to approach us and say, "We are not really equipped to help your son," the school blamed him for his struggles. And therefore, they blamed us. They had such a limited repertoire when it came to working with him. One of us would get a call: "He needs to get picked up." The first time there was an issue in Ohio, we got a call as well. This time, though, the message was, "We sent an extra aide into his classroom to help him out." I don't blame Blake for not having the personnel; I blame them for not recognizing that this lack was partially responsible for his struggles. He hated school. To this day, I'm not sure he's fully recovered.

As for me, there were a wide variety of concerns, all of them ones I was more than willing to own, even if I didn't always agree with them. I was struggling with when to be transparent versus when to keep my cards close to my chest. I was struggling with the notion of receiving feedback and then being discouraged from trying to address it. To me, this just promoted the triangular communication that made things difficult. Teachers could immediately go over my head. When I asked why they weren't being encouraged to talk to me first, that, too, was put on me. There must, I was told, be some reason they don't want to talk to you first. I was willing to accept that I was, as one of the mathematically inclined leaders was prone to saying, at least 51 percent responsible for everything involving me, but my conviction that the school promoted this kind of tattletale middle school communication culture never gained any traction except for among my peers.

And it was one of my peers, the kind recipient of my many rants, who was now becoming my supervisor.

I had been part of the team involved in the search, as had the head of school. Some accused him of conducting a sham, saying that he'd already made up his mind, and all of our meetings and interviews and research were all a cover story. Several people on the hiring team brought this concern to my attention. I am hopelessly naive when it comes to what people mistakenly call "politics."[85] As delicately as I could, I asked him about it and he dismissed it. And I believed him. I trusted the guy, and still do.

Anyway, here I was, enduring my annual beating at the hands of both the outgoing and incoming assistant heads of school, when I realized I was done. Apparently, and no one smelled a rat here, a number of female teachers (of course, unnamed and unnumbered) had recently called to complain about me. And because they had complained, my incoming supervisor believed the accusations to be true.[86] If you are wondering about the nature of those accusations, so am I. I was never told. I was just told that whatever was causing them had to stop.

For me, the comparison is this. Teachers are constantly told to give students rubrics up front. Students can't, the

---

85 You can't have that word. It still means something noble to me. It is so often used as a synonym for pettiness (as was the case here). And that's wrong. I'm not giving up that word.

86 This would become a recurring conversation during my next, lame duck year—for both me and several colleagues. Our supervisor tended to believe the first story he was told, a criticism he adamantly denied. He never figured out that I wasn't the only one who had this complaint. Since I was soon to be a lame duck, my colleagues and I realized I could be the spokesperson for our collective complaints.

cliche goes, hit a target they can't see or one that's constantly moving. Yet here I was being told to stop . . . something.

This is the one piece of criticism I wholeheartedly and categorically reject. Of course, like many others, including my two supervisors, I have my blind spots. But for the most part, I'm an equal opportunity asshole. There are things that research tells us, for example, about female teachers and their reaction to boy behavior, especially at the middle school level. And when the head of school was first giving me the run-down of the Upper School department, he noted how many part-time female teachers we had and asked me to consider whether that was a practice I wanted to continue. If I was unfair to anyone, or perceived to be unfair, it had nothing to do with them being female. It had everything to do with me having some criticisms of their work—the female teacher who had to leave parent conferences early because of a sick child (perfectly understandable) and told the secretary to let all the parents know (not understandable), the female teacher who told me certain things about her decision making and then didn't like seeing them reflected back to her in print, the female librarian who was one of the most resolutely insincere[87] and unhelpful colleagues I've ever met.

So when I started year five at Blake, somewhat ironically having been asked to mentor one of the new PK-12 chairs, I knew I was skating on the proverbial thin ice, an apt metaphor for hockey-obsessed Minnesota. And, like most other things that involve grace, coordination, and balance, I can't skate.

I tried to be positive. I showed up at meetings that weren't

---

87 Minnesota Nice—Think Bob Dylan, a Minnesotan—"They smile at your face, but behind your back they hiss." He knows.

mandatory and volunteered for extra responsibilities. I tried to cultivate a relationship with the new head of school but found that awkward. I even started in my sweet spot with a discussion of books, but it would be an understatement to say that we just didn't click. I found her to be something of an automaton. As I've mentioned, she clearly had either not been given the charge to form relationships or she was ignoring it. Or perhaps, like me, she just wasn't very good at it. She had her checklist, her formula, and she was going to stick to it no matter what. Perhaps I didn't hide my disdain very well.

It soon became clear that part of her formula was to say things publicly and then have the rest of us scramble to make them true. At an event at the University of Minnesota, she was asked about the gaps in the Upper School curriculum. Reportedly she said, "Computer Science," which was true because we didn't offer it, and ninth grade World Literature / World History, which wasn't true because we *did* offer it. This was brought to my attention because several of the teachers had been confronted with the statement in public, including one while he was out walking his dog. I took a deep breath and made an appointment to speak with her about it. One of the elements of forming relationships, I had been taught, was learning institutional history. I thought I might try to walk her through the last few years, including the History Day debacle. I made no impression. In any event, she (again, without consultation and very publicly) presented her plan and that became *the* plan.

In late October, there came the request for two appointments, the first (I only realized later because, as you've seen, I just don't think this way) was for the telltale Friday afternoon.[88] Anyway, I can't remember much of what was said other than a decision had been made not to offer me another contract. The head of school and the assistant head, if they'd had a script or a plan, fumbled their way through it. I stayed pretty calm until the head of school, who'd taken about four minutes to get to know me, started her "integrity" speech. If you don't know it, it goes something like this. "Yes, we're doing this in November, but we expect you to keep doing your job. What's at stake is whether we're able to let you finish the year and offer you a good recommendation." I had no real objections to my leadership abilities being questioned. But I was not going to have my integrity questioned, not by her. I made that quite clear. The assistant head, my one-time peer, felt badly, I think. He admitted later that they'd made a mess of the meeting.

Just as private schools try to keep salaries a secret, they try to keep contractual things secret as well. The claim is that it's for the employee's protection. Nonsense. They want everyone to think that the school is some kind of utopia, where no one quits or is fired; they just resign. I didn't want the Blakevine to control the narrative. I wanted to. I sent out emails to each division. I followed up in person with as many people as I could find, even some outside of my department, in the next few days.

The salary piece had already started to bubble up among my peers. There is this taboo about not discussing salary or asking about it. But we were all doing the same job. Though

---

88 For those who don't know, such meetings are often scheduled for Friday afternoons, so employees don't have much of an opportunity to do anything in the "going postal" spectrum.

we all brought different experience to the position, we should have been paid roughly the same. I was asked, so I volunteered my salary with no hesitation. Those who were staying could not address the problem unless they had the information. The administration was relying on the power of that taboo so we would not become organized. I'm not sure much came of the efforts to address the inequities, but it was definitely worth the effort. One possible downside of private schools—no unions.

As you know by now, I'd left schools before, but not like this. I tried to keep doing my job and tried to organize things for my successor, an easy and popular and almost certainly excellent choice, a teacher in the Upper School who had been asked to apply. I felt myself getting phased out of things, both officially and unofficially. I took more breaks to protect my mental health. I skipped the end-of-the-year ceremonies. I wrapped up accounts, turned in keys, the school credit card, and all sorts of other markers of my job. I was grateful that the then Upper School division director (now assistant head of school) did not force me to move my office in the last two months of the year. I wouldn't have moved anyway. I just would have moved out. Still, the vultures descended and the person scheduled to take over the space started doing some interior decorating. I didn't care too much. I was just trying to check all of the boxes before I left. I received compliments that I appreciated but never really understood about how I'd kept doing my job. I finally ran out of steam before the last PK-12 meeting. I could think of nothing, no agenda, no ideas, no farewell address. I canceled it. I attended graduation because I wanted to see the graduation of that eighth grade class I'd started with during that first, pneumonia-filled year.

In the meantime, I looked for jobs. A promised opportunity to switch to a teaching position at the Blake Upper School vanished thanks to more of the unspoken (to me) criticisms of others. I worked to renew my public school teaching license. Kirsten had always been head-hunted and now entertained offers with more seriousness. Cleveland and San Diego emerged as the two leaders.

We were flown to San Diego for her final interview. While she was at the final interview, I was driven around neighborhoods with an eye to where we might live. While I enjoyed the tour, by the time we got to a neighborhood I thought we could afford, we were a good forty-five minutes from the museum. I had one interview at a school that went well. I couldn't get over the fact that the school really did have its lockers outside. I mean, I'd seen that in movies.

But Kirsten preferred Cleveland, and so did I. I knew of its Rust Belt reputation, but it was greener than I'd imagined. Kirsten was offered the position of president and CEO at the Great Lakes Science Center in Cleveland, and I was on my way to a position at the high school in our new neighborhood, Shaker Heights High School. We'd heard all sorts of good things about both the schools and the neighborhood. It was time, once again, to move.

Rant: Spirit Week

I am, despite my grumpy reputation and somewhat serious disposition, all for school spirit. I thought

Baltimore City College High School did a great job at cultivating this spirit with its meaningful traditions and attention to alumni relations. Somewhere along the line, though, school spirit became something I don't understand.

Students (and teachers) are invited to dress a particular way for each day of the week leading up to Homecoming. (So we only have school spirit around athletics? I did manage to convince a department head at St. Paul to get T-shirts made for our IB Diploma students and have them recognized at an assembly. And I like sports.) A committee is convened, ideas are batted around, and a schedule is announced. Sometimes, the ideas are thoughtless. Write on a white T-shirt day? Boys signing girls' white T-shirts? Not a good look. I had no objections to sports uniform day, or whatever it was called, until a white teacher showed up in a basketball uniform and an Afro. But none of this answers the question: What the hell does any of this have to do with school spirit? Wear school colors, I get. Wear your team uniform to school, I get. Though I don't love them, I even get pep rallies. But "Dress Like Your Favorite Character"? What in the world does this do to promote school spirit? What really is school spirit?

I think it's pride in your school. Your school's team wins a game or the chess tournament. Or perhaps students volunteer together. Or beat a rival school at, well, anything. Or get recognized for a genuine accomplishment, like 100 percent college acceptance. There should be a culture of "we" when it comes to school pride, not "I." You know there's pride when students return after graduation because they liked being there. That school was a place that meant something to their lives, and filled with at least some of the people who were there who meant something to their lives at an important and turbulent time of their lives. I still go back to my high school. Something happened there that I think was good and meaningful and it had nothing to do with getting to wear my pajamas to school once a year.

In the scheme of things, is this such a big deal? Probably not. A triumph of the superficial over the substantial, but there are higher priorities, though it's hard to tell that to someone dressed as a friggin' Mouseketeer.

If I sound like I have all of the answers, I don't. That's the point of these rants. I don't have Seven Habits or Forty-Nine Techniques. I have twenty-five years and a lot of stories.

10
Shaker Heights High School
Shaker Heights, OH

As I sat in the teacher's lunch area waiting for my first meeting at Shaker Heights High School, I scanned the bulletin board. Someone had posted a long narrative joke involving carnal relationships between various religious figures and animals. It was not a good first impression. Who put that up there? What made that person think it was OK? Who, prior to me, had seen it and left it there?

When I found my way into the English department office to meet some people, I was handed a copy of the SLO, an assessment required by the state of Ohio as part of the teacher's evaluation. I can never remember whether it counts as 35 percent or 50 percent; I think it's the latter. SLO stands for Student Learning Objective, and the fact that it can be abbreviated as SLO is an endless source of amusement for many. You can either use a vendor assessment (one premade by one of the many companies profiting by selling tests to public schools) or you can make your own. Shaker had elected to make its own.

As I read the one for the eleventh grade, I was incredulous. Part of it was based on a book I'd read many times and taught several times, Chinua Achebe's *Things Fall Apart*. And there were multiple choice questions about the book based on the most trivial minutiae imaginable. I couldn't even begin to guess at the answers; nor did I care. I scoffed. As with the joke in the staff room, it was not a good first impression. I mean both the test and my scoff.

But that was only the beginning of the end of the department's obsession with multiple choice questions. They spent as much time mocking standardized tests as they spent making them. If the Scantron machine went down in the department office, there was a reaction akin to a national emergency. Multiple choice tests were, one department member told me, the thing to do in public education. My way of teaching, I was told later, was more collegiate. I was called a "journeyman"[89] teacher.

For some indefensible reason, likely related to the district's efforts to accommodate everyone's interests, the eleventh grade class I taught, the one where I'd be teaching *Things Fall Apart*, mixed both honors and college prep students. The college prep designation was, naturally, abbreviated as CP. Students, as they are wont to do, soon decided that it really stood for "colored people." They knew. Parents knew. Everyone knew. I was present when the superintendent first found out. Sometimes jaws really do drop.

Tracking begins in fifth grade in the district, and despite the claims of many, the true integration in the schools—and these are the words of a central office administrator—"is in the hallways." I was given advice about how to counsel students to demote themselves from honors to college prep. It was made very clear to me which students should receive such guidance.

---

89 I wanted to respond with the line from *The Princess Bride*—"I don't think that word means what you think it means"—but the person who used it, well, he wasn't worth the limited energy I had left for the place.

When it came time for the semester exam, I was asked to submit my exam for the class to our department head, a not unreasonable request. I cut and pasted multiple choice questions from someone else's exam and then spent time crafting the essay portion, making distinctions between what was expected from college prep students and what was expected from honors students. This conversation ensued:

Department head: Both groups have the same number of multiple choice questions.
Me: Yes, but the written portion was different—length, how many stories they have to consider, the rubric.
Department head: The honors students need to have more multiple choice questions.
Me: Oh.

I think I mustered about ten more multiple choice questions; it was painful.

The ninth grade curriculum was not a curriculum. It was a series of books, weighed down by the ever-present and ever-unnecessary research paper. And the first book was, largely because of one teacher's obsession with it, *Great Expectations*. Now don't get me wrong; I love the book. But here, welcome to high school, now read *Great Expectations*. Really? When I wondered aloud about the appropriateness and timing of the selection, the department head said I could move it to anywhere in the first semester because it was on the first semester exam. Great. The summer reading was *The House of the Scorpion*—a great book, complete with stickers on the front signifying its awards, though perhaps a little low level for many of the students. Two of the students of color, however, showed up having been told to read *Miracle's Boys* by Jacqueline Woodson. Over 200 pages shorter, *Miracle's Boys* (which has an award sticker of its own) tells the story of three African-American brothers who have lost their parents and must make it in New York City on their own. This is complicated by the return of the middle brother's return from jail. *Scorpion* is a dystopian story run by the drug baron, El Patron.[90] Cultural competency, anyone? And to follow either one with Dickens?

The summer reading for the eleventh grade was *City of Thieves*, a book chosen, I was told, for its appeal to boys, something that did turn out to be true. The book was a bit meta for some students; there is a character named David in the introduction, and the author's name is David. There is also a main Jewish character who is, for no literary reason I could recognize, pretty obsessed with the size of his nose. When I mentioned aloud in the English office that I found the book mildly anti-Semitic, our department head flatly declared, with her George W. Bush-style logic, "It's not anti-Semitic." And that, apparently, was that.

I liked that I was teaching both a ninth grade class and a twelfth grade one. I enjoyed seeing the full range. The seniors, when I checked on their college search process, said their goal was ABC. Anywhere but Cleveland. The ninth graders were

---

90 In truth, both *could* be fine choices. They could be fine choices if someone, say a department chair, was paying attention to the big picture. As far as I could tell, *Scorpion* was not balanced with any other pieces of Latin American fiction. There were other African-American stories. One was set in a Chicago ghetto. The other was about slavery.

young and generally well prepared. There was a prevailing sense of entitlement among the students. And the staff, for that matter. Everyone believed the headlines. "Shaker is a great school, therefore we are great students and teachers." I was reminded of a talk I'd heard in Minnesota. A new head of school had told his teachers not to be so proud of making eagles out of their students. After all, the parents handed over eagle eggs. The same is true in Shaker. At least the white half. The measure of success for that school should be how the other Shaker performs.

Once the year began, I couldn't stop running into stupid. It was like it had a homing device for me. More likely, though, it was yet another case of me having a knack for it. A woman came to the door one day and said she was there to pick up a student. Now I knew the student took a van somewhere for some special program I've since forgotten, so I knew this was likely to be true. I didn't, however, know this woman.

Me: Do you have any ID?
Her: I left it. Everyone knows me. I've been doing this forever.
Me: Well, I'm new, so if you could get something, someone to vouch for you.
Her (walking away): Just get the kid ready.
Me: I don't work for you.

And naturally, since she, like many of the folks at Blake, had a middle school mentality when it came to communication, told my department head who accepted her version of it as fact.

Another. There was an abbreviated schedule for some reason. I gave the class over to some reading time as they were having trouble getting through the Dickens. The guidance counselor sent two students back to class with one minute remaining. I opened the door, showed them where I'd posted the reading for the next day, and said that they might as well go on to their next class. This, too, proved to be an appalling move on my behalf, though to her credit, the guidance counselor found her way to forgive me, and I found her easy to work with after that.

I was caught up in the stress of the move and did not feel healthy much of the time. My knees were hurting. I remember distinctly stopping in the front hall, bent over from the pain and wondering if I could even keep walking. I could and did, but I probably should have listened more to my body.

The school nicely sent me to the National Council of Teachers of English conference in Boston along with two other teachers. I don't remember one of them, but the other, as far as her teaching skills, she made really good bulletin boards. She was certified in grades 4-9, an inane Ohio arrangement, which made her of limited use in the department. But, like I said, she made really good bulletin boards.

We both went to the same session, though at the time, I didn't know she was there. I brought up what I perceived to be idiocy of the *Great Expectations* selection during the question and answer period. Naturally, that got reported back too.

It goes on. Generally, schools have the policy of not moving students because of conflicts with the teacher, a policy that except in the most extreme cases, makes sense to me. But Shaker, I soon learned, was ruled (and remains ruled) by the parents who pick up the phone and know who to call. Thus, without even a parent conference with me or any consultation, one student was moved at the semester break. The parent, it turned out, was very close with, you guessed it, the department head. Entitlement. Still, like I said, I couldn't get away from stupid.

The cliched final straw came early in the second semester. Without being given any reason, I was told that I was no longer to be on the eleventh grade team, but on the ninth grade team. This was fine with me, as at least two members of the eleventh grade team confused the word "meeting" with the word "complaining," and I had little patience for that. Later, I was told, there had been complaints so that had been the reason for the move. This, of course, was never explained to me.

Both the department head and the principal had an aversion to difficult conversations. The association rep would later say he'd been aware of the problems all along, but couldn't really answer why he'd never shared any concerns with me. The department head, I was told, insisted she had been very clear with me that things had become serious. In retrospect, I remembered a comment from her to the effect of , "I think I need to pull back from working with you." Even if that was it, I asked once I learned my job was at stake, shouldn't something which has such serious consequences be put in writing? Again, no answer.

The principal, who would resign a year or maybe two later,[91] was also reluctant to say difficult things. He had said to me at post-conference that one element of the rubric could "get in my way." I agreed that it was an area I need to work on, and devised and began to execute a plan that he approved.

---

91 Even I could see it coming.

Through all of this, I got to know and enjoy my students. I tend to think of student growth as kind of like watching a Polaroid develop. At first, the ninth graders are amorphous blobs of color. By senior year, they are sharply rendered, much more distinct. I'm pretty certain many of the students would go on to do impressive things in college and in whatever field they chose. For some, the biggest challenge seemed to be how to find a parking spot near the school without getting a ticket. They were going to do great things because they were expected to do great things and entitled to do them. I'm not claiming their lives were utopian, or that I even knew too many details of many of their lives. But the students and their families claimed their futures as their right, not necessarily as something to be earned. I wasn't unhappy as much as I was just plain uneasy. The place and I? We just didn't fit.

And then, for some reason, I got way too intense about an issue at one of those ninth grade meetings. The meeting was a regular event and, at a previous one, I felt comfortable approaching one of them about my discomfort. She apologized in person and followed up with a note. The others, including the teacher heretofore known as Bulletin Board, well, I just didn't want to deal with them.

During one of my planning periods, the department head asked me to explain what was going on in the ninth grade meetings, so I retreated to my classroom to get the document that had been the source or excuse for my intensity.. I brought it back to the English office and was going over it with her when another teacher, one I cared for neither personally nor professionally, thought it appropriate to interject, and I snapped at her. Based on conversations with her and overhearing her (I couldn't avoid it; she used the English office as her therapy sessions), I had no respect for this woman. She'd been a late part-time hire, and such people are who they are. Late in the hiring process, you have to take who you can get. Apparently, she left the English office distraught and in tears. I went into her classroom, waited until she had given instructions, and apologized to her. I returned to the English office, told the department head I'd apologized, and went on with my day.

I would later be handed a copy of the report the department head made to the administration of the building and district, but not me. I had asked very early in the year whether she was a part of my evaluation and she'd said, unequivocally, no. The principal, I was told, would be doing my evaluations. I was later told that of course she'd be evaluating my contributions to the department and that I should have known that . . . somehow. This incident, naturally, she put in writing.

Now, I've always been taught that such reports are to be fact-based, or at least fact-based in one section and then opinion-based. Her report was, as the movies sometimes say, "based on true events" and loaded with such hyperbolic language as to render it amateurish or at least open to question. But once again, without even a consultation with me (it was probably too late by then), it was accepted as fact. My fate, I was told, was being discussed. The association rep, suddenly my constant companion, told me I'd likely receive a "verbal verbal." That was really the name of it. I still find that funnier than SLO. I went home for the weekend expecting it to come the following week.

That Saturday I drove to Columbus to see a student of mine compete in the Poetry Out Loud state finals. On

Sunday, I went to hear another student play with the youth symphony. As instructed, I checked in with the association rep before the concert began. The situation, I was informed, had grown more serious; my job was at stake. I was to prepare a list of my contributions because the union rep and the principal would be going to see someone in the central office (who would later tell me that the principal wanted me out) to make the case for my contract to be renewed. I left the concert at intermission.

I had, at previous schools, always taken some pride in finishing my job well, regardless of the circumstances of my departure.[92] This time, not so much. I largely put things in cruise control and got myself through the year. I'm glad I didn't end up staying there. I still do think I deserved another year. I spent probably too much time dwelling on it and poking about for some clarity, but over time, I let it go . . . mostly. I was not that sad about being told, for the second consecutive year, that I had to resign. I'd never felt comfortable there. I did start to wonder, obsess over the prospect that they were right. Two schools with excellent reputations had arrived at the same conclusion; I wasn't welcome. Maybe, I thought and wrote in long emails to friends and family, something had passed me by, that teaching had become something that as no longer suited for me, or I had become no longer suited for it. Maybe I should get the message and find something else to do. I was discouraged, demoralized, just plain down.

And then Kirsten, once again, helped me find the way.

----

92 See Blake section.

Rant: Traditions

As of this writing, my son Ezra is starting his fifth grade year, and two so-called traditions have come up that trouble me a great deal.

Please don't get me wrong. I like traditions. When they make sense. When everyone involved in them can explain their origin. Baltimore City College High School was great at this. The Blake School was not. And people who adhere to traditions resent questions about them.

Now, I think I've mentioned before, and I'm sure I'll mention again, that part of the problem here is my tone, both real and perceived. I can ask people the time and find a way to offend them. So when I ask people about their traditions, sometimes because I'm curious and sometimes because I'm trying, in my unsubtle way, to make a point, I can definitely offend them.

Recently, I attended an open house at our son's school. Kirsten is a paperwork wizard. Just as she finished the epic amount of paperwork for all of the various camps, on came the blizzard of paperwork for school. Since I'm often busy with my beginning of the school year events, those generally fall to her as well. So when I saw an opportunity to take one Brussel sprout[93] off of her plate, I volunteered to go solo.

To their credit, Ezra's teachers had everything organized. I collected my paperwork and found a

---

93   Bad metaphor. We like Brussels sprouts.

seat. His team of teachers seems fine, enthusiastic, and perhaps a bit too focused on themselves as performers. I paged through the materials and winced at the poorly written sections, the grade penalties for late work, and cringed when I heard the teachers use some form of the word "rigor" a half dozen times. They seemed proud that their classes were the same as the regular classes though, they assured us, the classes would still count as enriched because they would move through the material faster. "That's not enriched," I wanted to say, "that's just faster." It reminded me of one of the math teachers at Hume-Fogg. He used to boast about how many math problems he gave the students to do, a task they deserved, he was certain, because they were at the academic magnet school. "More," I wanted to say, "is not the same as more challenging. It's just more." In every case where—either as a teacher or a parent—I've encountered any form of tracking, the teachers always make it clear that the classes should come with warning labels saying, "This class is not suitable for everyone." It's a ridiculous sort of perverse pride. When I queried our daughter's fifth grade "enriched" English teachers about the workload, they suggested, as though reading from a well-worn script, that perhaps she wasn't used to being held accountable and wasn't up to an enriched class.

"No," I wanted to say, "we just think asking fifth graders to do three different things at once is stupid." What is the point of these open houses? Do I want to meet these teachers? Sure. Do I want to be given papers that are recycled from year to year and performances by teachers that are nothing akin to how they actually teach? Do I want to be treated like a sheep? We were told at Ezra's open house that if the two teachers decided that our children didn't belong in enriched classes that we should just trust them. "Uh . . . no," I wanted to say.[94]

Let's not just do things a certain way because that's the way they've always been done. Ask the "why" questions. If the answer is that it's required, then fine, say that. But don't just blindly follow tradition for its own sake.

---

94 But I didn't. Maybe I am finally maturing. Or maybe I knew my son would kill me if he knew I said that.

11
John F. Kennedy 2.0
Cleveland, OH

When we first arrived in Cleveland, Kirsten participated in a program called Leadership Cleveland. She loved it and met a lot of great people during her year with the program, including a woman who was in charge of hiring for the Cleveland schools. After Kirsten told her about my situation, she kindly invited me to her at her house one morning, and we had a long talk. Her instructions for me were to get in touch with a principal at a new public school that was just starting. I did, and we met in a coffee shop adjacent to a cathedral on the campus of Cleveland State University. After about four minutes with this new principal, I knew that whatever she was doing, I wanted to be a part of it.

The head of school I liked and respected at Blake used to tell us to look for people who got our blood racing, who got us excited about teaching. This new principal was like that for me. It felt like, at least from my end, that we could talk for hours. She must have felt pretty positive about the conversation, too, because she hired me. I was energized in a way I hadn't been in a long while. I was part of a team that was doing something I'd long dreamed of: We were making a school. We made plans. We had arguments. We went zip lining.

And then everything changed.

***

John F. Kennedy, or JFK, was, we were told, a failing school. We would be one of the small schools replacing it. We were to be phased in year by year as the original incarnation was being phased out. For two years, we would be located in a former elementary school that was not even in Cleveland, but in a neighboring suburb called Garfield Heights. We were calling ourselves JFK 2.0.

There was no clearer indication of the original school's failures than the visual our campus coordinator pointed out to me when we went to "the big school" for a pep rally. The ninth grade (ourselves and the other new JFK 2.0 incarnation) took up four bleachers. The tenth grade (still members of the original version) took up three, the eleventh grade, two, and the twelfth grade (some of whom were part of the pep rally) barely took up one. The image was clear. Students were starting at the school; they just weren't finishing. Our principal, a student of social replication theory, was confident that we could avoid this pitfall using the model she'd developed. She was smart, charismatic, and inspirational. We believed in her. We thought she was right.

She had this conception of time that was and remains as mind-blowingly radical as it is simple. If a student needs a school year and two months to do algebra, why shouldn't he have it? If a student needs an hour rather than fifty-two minutes to complete a writing assignment, why shouldn't she have it? Students at JFK 2.0 were not going to fail; they were going to receive incompletes. Failures made students drop out. Incompletes kept doors open. I've since been told I have a "healthy disregard for the traditional Carnegie Unit," and I'm okay with that. It's random and it doesn't work. Why does a student have to master a subject by a date that the district determines? Isn't the priority that they master the subject, not that they master it before winter break?

At the school we were building, students would have more control over their schedules. There would be certain "musts," and teachers could "claim" students they needed to see, but then advisors would, on a weekly basis (changed to monthly during our second year) help students fill in the remainder of their schedule. A portion of the curriculum was going to be given over to online learning. Because I am a card-carrying Luddite, I wasn't sure about this part. But I knew something had to be different.

Ours would be a year-round school. Summer slide, for our students—who didn't really have much access to summer enrichment opportunities—would be minimized. Ten weeks on; three weeks off (for the students; two for us). We would do our best to keep students in school by means of restorative justice. (This was the first I'd heard of this concept, at least as it relates to schools.) We would be a 1:1 school. That is, there would be one computer for every student. Students would be able to take their computers home. An extended absence would not cause students to fall behind. Perhaps most radically and definitely most importantly was something that required neither technology nor money. We were charged with the urgency of forming relationships with our students. This notion was not new; the urgency of it was.

If all of this seems idyllic, it was. We would learn both by experience and by visiting other schools that we'd bitten off quite a lot, and this was even before the students showed up.

We were an interesting group. It took my new humanities colleagues about eight minutes to demonstrate more emotional intelligence than I had in the last twenty years. The music teacher was not just a jack-of-all-trades in the way that all arts teachers are pretty much required to be, but an inspiration. He taught the faculty how to play a drumline during our opening week, and soon produced an outstanding student drumline, a place that became a kind of home to at least a few students who had nowhere else to shine.

I was to share a room with the social studies teacher. We had flexible furniture, but that was not enough. The students were not as small as the ones who had once inhabited these primary school rooms; nor, I suspect, were they as polite. We had a common area that we called the Eagle's Nest. We didn't have many books, but I was working on that. We had everything we needed, we thought, except for students.

And then they came.

***

The first challenge was that the students came and the computers still hadn't made an appearance. That was probably because of a woefully understaffed technology department in the district office and the glacial pace of moving a purchase through the district's bureaucracy. So for a few weeks, we were a school that featured an online curriculum, but had no way to get the students online.

Other challenges soon revealed themselves. We had, unknowingly, recruited students from two different gang areas. Conflicts soon arose, and the police soon became regular visitors. The more popular ones would be greeted with waves and smiles.

Since the school was located in a residential area, we were concerned about maintaining good relationships with our neighbors. The administration would always walk the students to the bus stop, a place that also became a location for conflicts. One day, early in the year, I joined them. I was, shall we say, *surprised* by the number of police cars in the area of the bus stop. I was trailing one of my advisees by maybe fifty yards, when one officer put on his siren, drove in front of her, and got out. He was large, taller than me (and I'm 6' 2") and white (I am, too). He was wearing a bulletproof vest and was very definitely invading her personal space. I couldn't hear what he was saying, but he was animated enough that his face was turning red. Finally, he dismissed her with a disdainful wave of the hand, and she continued on her way to the bus stop. I approached him gingerly and identified myself.

"I'm her advisor," I said. "Can you tell me what she did wrong so I can talk with her about it?"

"She was jaywalking," the officer replied.

This was the first in a confluence of things. I was reading Michelle Alexander's book *The New Jim Crow* at the time.[95] I'd heard her speak before and thought, "OK, I get the point here," but I'd underestimated her. The book awakened synapses I'm not sure I knew I had. And with this incident, it all started to click into place.

---

95 If you haven't read it, put this book down and go read it. It's urgent. Then come back to this one.

We taught two different kinds of classes that first year—a workshop (more skills-based, a kind of partner for the online program) and a seminar (a discussion-based class that was much more in my comfort zone). I was trying out ideas with the students, to get to know them and to begin to figure out what interested them. I raised the prospect of exploring the idea of justice. It is generally an attractive topic for teens. One student raised his hand. "Can we talk about the cops?"

A few weeks later, we all knew the name Mike Brown.

Something was happening to me.

***

The computers finally arrived, and one of my advisees was the first to be caught viewing pornography. This would be the beginning of a recurring conflict between the school and he and his father. We implemented our fluid time schedule, but student attendance was erratic. Our main math teacher, who was reportedly very knowledgeable about math, proved even more prone to alienating people (both students and peers) than I usually was. The "college and careers" person was stirring up union related issues with respect to our schedule, and in this way, she was alienating the administration *and* her colleagues. It was dizzying. There were adults imploding, and for maybe the first time none of them were me.

In the classroom, I was learning that our students didn't tend to read— some because they didn't like to and some because they couldn't. Others weren't even able to try because we had few books to offer them. I was working on that. They didn't write much either, but a few did. Three of them asked me about forming a poetry club, and we began to meet regularly. I gave them a writing prompt, and we all wrote and shared and commented. The quietest among them wanted to have an open mic. I didn't think we were ready, nor did we have enough people. We were supposed to promote student voices, though, so I cleared it and made the arrangements. It was awesome. It became a monthly tradition. I started to investigate Cleveland's spoken word community.

The online component of our curriculum, though, was a disappointment. It already seemed clear to me that Edgenuity, the program we'd chosen, had done little to take advantage of being online. They had simply inhaled a pretty standard textbook and placed it online. All of it. There was too much for students to do, so we cut it down. Students were cheating, so we worked to combat that. Re-takes were being given out like free pens at the bank, so our two Edgenuity coaches created a policy. There were an endless series of speed bumps, including access to working computers and keeping those computers charged. We'd assigned each student a laptop and recorded that number, but we hadn't made an effort to keep track of chargers. They became black market currency. Students hoarded them; we would find a dozen at a time in a locker. We were forever chasing things, but we were given the freedom to figure it out, and it was exciting. When the work became too consuming for both us and the students, we were coached to devise ways to scale it back.

I was always going to be more interested in the seminar part of the work anyway. And I was finally ready. It was time to talk about cops. Mostly, I listened. The students had such incredible stories, more about small, everyday incidents than I anticipated.

Very few of them reported any large dramas (something that would change over the next two years), but they all had stories. I brought in guests—representatives from a Cleveland group working against mass incarceration, the ACLU, and because my principal rightly prodded me, the police. We went through a variety of police officers. I hadn't thought that I was putting them through a try-out them until the officer I finally chose called me out on it. She said she knew she was being "auditioned." The police tended to be straightforward, the kids a bit shy. (The first question, after all of that anger and all of those stories, "Do you have a police dog?")

I generated interest and engagement, but I didn't know what to do with it. I extended the seminar. (They were only supposed to last a week.) I created a presentation assignment. The students knew less about PowerPoint than I did. My colleagues were as patient with my ineptitude as they were with sharing the limited number of computers that had finally arrived. The few students brave enough to stand up there with largely incomplete PowerPoints had only a basic level of understanding of the issues and very little by way of action steps. It ended with a thud. But as more and more cops rotated through the building to talk with and sometimes take away our students, I knew I had to try it again. And then two more words entered the national vocabulary, two words that struck close to home: Tamir Rice.

***

November. A bit of snow on the ground. A boy, who would become Mr. Rice in police accounts, is playing at a rec center. He is playing with a toy gun. There are cameras. We know this. He seems to menace passersby, though none of them show any real signs of alarm; none call the police. Instead, a man across the street does. He emphasizes, repeatedly, that the gun might be fake. This information gets lost in transmission. The dispatcher sends a car, containing a rookie who sought a job in Cleveland so he could have more "action" and his mentor, an older officer who was driving. Perhaps because their understanding is that Tamir (always Tamir in my book) might be taking his gun and heading into the rec center, they hop a curb and skid to a stop in front of him. The rookie, in the passenger seat, claims he says, "Hands up!" three times in two seconds. Go ahead. Get a stopwatch. Try it. I'll wait.

We can see on the video that Rice's hand moves in the direction of his waistband and then the police car blocks our view. And then Tamir is shot and lying there, and the officers do nothing to assist him. And then his sister rushes to be near him and is placed in the back of the police car that skidded to a stop. There are more details after this, but the key one is this: Tamir Rice, age twelve, is dead.[96]

The students, perhaps some of them posing, were not surprised. But for me, for me, the world as I knew it was shifting under my feet. I had these feelings that I didn't have words for. I was angry and wanted to do something, but those were not new instincts for me. I was flailing—professionally, emotionally, politically, you name it. Just flailing.

One of the many new things I had to get used to in Cleveland was the transience. Students would show up, then

---

96 Start here (http://www.cleveland.com/court-justice/index.ssf/2017/01/tamir_rice_shooting_a_breakdow.html). I can't watch it anymore.

we wouldn't see them for a while. We'd learn weeks later that they'd transferred. Or we'd learn that they were incarcerated. Some names would stay on our computer files. Some names would disappear. Other names would come back. We'd learn not to throw anything away.

There was a name that lingered on my advisory list for the entire first quarter.

I knew nothing about him. A few students seemed to know of him. He was absent for the first ten weeks. I had to mark him absent every day. His name never disappeared. He was still enrolled at our school. But where was he?

We were too busy trying to make it through each school day, so none of us looked into it too deeply. And then he showed up, a few days into the second quarter. I learned that he liked math and had trouble with vision in one eye. And then suddenly, he was gone again. Arrested. The police from my own neighborhood apparently monitored attendance, and when he was finally not marked absent, they showed up to collect him. They asked the principal if she wanted them to parade him around the school as an example. She said, in no uncertain terms, "No."

I'd just met him and he was gone. I took it personally. He was on my advisory list, and I wanted him back.

And so in I went. Into the labyrinth of the juvenile justice system. A book I'd read, Nell Bernstein's *Burning Down the House*, had argued that one of the key things to getting juveniles through a period of incarceration was for them to maintain a connection with the outside world. I stopped by the police station to find out what my student had done and learned not only what he'd done, but also what had been done to him and his family. I learned that it was true that the police monitored social media.

It's always amazing to me how quickly it happens to me, especially since I have switched schools so often, but I love my students. I'm not always so great at saying it, but the love only increases as I learn more about them. The response to a student like this was, I thought, to love harder.

I showed up at court hearing. I got to know his probation officer and his mother. Once, as I waited to go into a hearing, I glanced out the majestic window past the ramshackle building that advertised help with bonds and saw a billboard looming Eckleburg-like over the entrance to what I understood to be a predominantly African-American neighborhood. "Get tested," it urged those driving by. "Do your children have lead poisoning?" "Is there lead in your home?" Estimates for testing the building I was in ranged from $4-$10 million. And the city wanted its residents to get their homes and children tested on their own?

I was introduced to a new genre of writing, one not covered by the Common Core: the letter to the judge. I went to visit my student at the alternative program where he'd been placed. I arranged with a local restaurant dedicated to re-entry for him to have an interview.[97] I wrote a letter weekly and then I got a bit antsy and switched to using the school address as my return address.

I was appalled by the facility where he'd been placed. I mean, the conditions seemed to be fine, but the people

---

97 Here: http://www.cleveland.com/dining/index.ssf/2013/10/edwins_restaurant_ outreach_to.html

and the program were awful. They wanted him to not only be converted, but to like it. They manipulated him (and, presumably, all of their "residents") like a puppet. There were these levels. If he got to a certain level, he would be allowed to try a short period of time at home. He was close to it. And then he wasn't. I learned that from a letter he sent and contacted the probation officer who contacted the director of the facility for an update. The director then called me *three times* the next day to harangue me for my interference. At the next hearing, I made sure the judge knew that.

Eventually, he was released from the facility and returned to school. And all, briefly, was well. And then he started arriving a bit late each day. I drove him to his required meetings with his probation officer, but I started hearing about some comments he was making and the way he was flashing money. He wouldn't give me his cell phone number. He was speaking to female teachers in an inappropriate way. He stole a classmate's bus card. And then he was gone. On the run. And then he was arrested again. My colleagues expected he and his mother to reach out for help again. They didn't, but his probation officer did. I told him that I wasn't going to commit as much time to trying to help him. The last I saw of him was in a text message someone forwarded to me. He was pointing a gun at the camera.

Did I do the wrong thing? Should I have let things take their course, perhaps invested my time in someone more interested in finding his way out of a situation? If I'd stayed out of it, would he have been rehabilitated to some version of a decent life? I have no way of knowing. But I am as certain as I can be of this. Right now, the justice system, the way it's set up is, at its core, racist. (And not because of "bad apples.") Mass incarceration is not an accident. It's what the system was set up to do, and it's working perfectly. You'll have a hard time convincing me that it's ever a good place for an African-American male to be.

***

Something unexpected seemed to happen to me that first year. I became a kind of elder statesmen. I promised by humanities colleagues that I wouldn't play the "I have more experience" card too often, and I think I honored that promise. But another colleague, our college and careers counselor, was publicly taking potshots at everyone and becoming a big part of our problem. And here I was, a year after being told for the second consecutive year (and school) that I was the problem, being asked to talk with her in order to mediate. It was an odd view, being on that side of the table. It made me realize how I must have looked at the end of my time at Blake and at Shaker. I felt sorry for her, but I was learning to like my new side of the table.

The only thing harder than the first year of a new school, our principal kept telling us, was the second year. We would add another grade, which would require us to add new teachers as well. For some reason, the principal could step outside of the normal hiring requirements for the first year. After that, however, we had to follow the union process. On paper, it looked like we only had one problem—science. But that was a gross underestimation of our problems. While we waited for the others to emerge, it turned out that the one problem we knew about was a very big problem indeed.

Before the year even started, I was sitting next to him in a staff meeting when he referred to the female students at his previous school as "bitches and hoes." I could feel the glare of the spotlight turn on him. I edged my chair away. I didn't want to be caught in the mental photographs people were making of this moment. As soon as the year began, we began to hear complaints from the students. They had a video of him sleeping in class. He had told the students that he used to sell crack. And then he just stopped showing up. When he did show up, he seemed hungover and was definitely disheveled. I learned that his mother was sick, but that didn't explain it all. He was shifted to a science support position, and thus we began a series of long-term science teacher subs. I'd usually find out their names from the students right before they were replaced.

The second personnel issue that showed up was our Teach for America (TFA) hire. I am not against Teach for America. I even contemplated applying once upon a time. I'm not so sold on teacher preparation programs and certification necessarily being better than alternative paths, like TFA. We need to make it easier for second career folks to find their way into the classroom. Unfortunately, in this particular case, our TFA hire was woefully unprepared. She was assigned to a challenging place—the ED, or "emotionally disturbed" classroom—so maybe we set her up to struggle. But I also struggled with her on a personal level and, in general, found her very, very[98] young.

Things did not improve when she was moved to the English Intervention Specialist position during our second

---

[98] ery

year and the school's third. Then, of course, I had to work more closely with her. She seemed to be trying to position herself as a leader without realizing she just didn't have the skills, experience, or credibility to stake that kind of claim. At meetings, she acted like someone had elected her spokesperson. She was forever going on trainings, and when she was at school she handled her students in a woefully naive way. When something went haywire, and I lost track of how many times it did, she would take full advantage of the union's provisions and take the allotted days off to "recover" from the traumatic situation that she may have been unprepared to handle. I tried speaking to her supervisor, but nothing changed.

The personnel problems continued. A female social studies teacher, mired a bit in a personal situation, had some trouble grasping the way the school was supposed to work and offered to switch places with the new African-American male social studies teacher, who had been hired to be the learning coach. I took that as a moment of panic and didn't think much of it. I should have.

To this day, I'm not really sure what went wrong for her during her first year (the school's second). She did not get along with the founding social studies teacher, and some racial tension developed—words said in the staff room, that kind of thing. I was never around when it happened, but I was not pleased that our principal seemed to be trying to solve it by email. When I tried to provide some suggestions, I was told, curtly, to "stay in my lane."

The principal had told me once that she saw as her barometer our energetic young math teacher. "If we lose him," she would say, "then we know we're not doing this right." What I never managed to say to her was that we *were* losing him. He frequently vented his frustration to me. I tried to straddle that line between maintaining his trust in me and alerting her that she was "losing the locker room." It didn't work. The math teacher transferred after that year.

In the meantime, my teaching was getting much better. I've never been much of a team-teacher, but I was paired with the woman who had been the English and Social Studies learning coach the year before. After a while of trying to run two different classes, we realized that we were both working on similar topics, both related to food, and started collaborating more openly.

Prior to our third quarter, a few things happened. First, we got a donation of sixty-three copies of the Sharon Draper novel *Tears of a Tiger,* and tickets for that many students to hear her in person. More importantly, though, we were given time to plan under the direction of two people—one an employee of the district and one a hired consultant and we took advantage of it.[99]

And it clicked. She had her strengths. She was good with technology, committed to one-on-one conferencing (she'd have four people lined up and I'd be waving my arms saying, "No waiting!" to no avail), and much more aware of the students' culture than the rest of us. She was an amazingly engaging and dramatic reader, and she was much more adept at using humor to defuse situations with students than I was. Me? I was good at backwards planning, making handouts,

---

99 I think there's a mathematical formula out there explaining the relationship between the amount of complaints a teacher makes about the lack of time to talk with other teachers and how much of that time he wastes.

and sequencing lessons. And that was probably it. We stopped taking our free periods and alternated who would take the lead. Whoever was secondary would deal with discipline or conference quietly with those students in need of help.

It was during that quarter when we received two of my favorite compliments of all time. The principal came to observe one day and said she'd be pleased to put her daughter in our class. A representative of one of our funders came to watch the day before spring break, and he asked the principal, "Do your English teachers know that it's the last day before break?" If memory serves, she responded with something like, "They're on a roll." And we were. Even the students started saying things about how well we were working together. It was fun. And we were doing good work. The number of assignments students were turning in went way up and the number of them that were indications of mastery followed suit.

It felt like it was all coming together. But with a single departure, it was about to start coming apart.

***

I've never liked the, "Can you see me in my office later?" request from a supervisor, and my principal knew me well enough to follow it up with, "It's nothing bad." And so, when I next had time, I went to see her. She told me was leaving for another job. The new position at a local university sounded perfect for her, and I was happy for her. Well, I'd like to believe that I was at least 60 percent happy for her. And the other 40 percent? It was a strange feeling. I was disappointed. Deflated. I'm not sure. I was a little angry. If you start a high school, I thought, you should at least stay four years to see one class all the way through. The next year would make me a hypocrite.

We all waited for news of our new principal. We were all disappointed but unsurprised that none of us was included in the process. Then one day he showed up accompanied by an administrator who'd promised the year before that we'd be seeing a lot of him. My co-teacher had to remind me who he was.

I would eventually have some one-on-one time with the new principal. Later, I was told that he was advised to do that having been informed that if he wanted to be accepted by the staff, he had to be accepted by me. The conversation felt odd to me, like an interview after the barn door had closed, if I may be permitted to mix a metaphor. Still, I can't deny that I came out of the interview feeling positive. He was energetic, positive, and eager to please. He mentioned Kierkegaard. Maybe my guard was down, I don't know. I thought things were going to be okay.

The next school year would bring the inevitable move to the original John F. Kennedy High School building. We had outgrown our original space. This had always been the plan. There was, in fact, talk of a newer building being constructed for us. I think the ground has finally been broken on that project.

I was glad to have more space, though not so glad that the co-teaching arrangement would be no more. I was to follow our original group of students and take the eleventh grade. My former co-teacher would take tenth, and a new hire would take the ninth grade. He seemed friendly enough. Organized. Test-obsessed. Another former administrator. We also had a new Humanities Learning Coach who seemed great. Having been treated extremely poorly by her math/science colleague (our original math teacher, now being hidden in the right field coaching role because of his consistent inability to connect with students) and perhaps not that well-supported by the rest of us, busily trying to adjust to the new principal and the new building, she didn't last long. She was offered a more standard technology-based position elsewhere and she wisely took it. That was disappointing, but not a cause for panic. A familiar long-term sub returned. He was suited for the coaching position, less because of his humanities skills than because he understood the role and was eager and organized and wanted to do it well. He had a good rapport with the students. But I'm getting ahead of myself.

The new principal had, as many administrators do, a barrel full of initiatives. I can't remember the name of the first one that infuriated me,[100] but it was essentially a positive behavior system. A committee would decide on positive and negative behaviors and award each one either positive or negative points. At regular intervals, we would stop, look at the totals, and allow the students who had them to spend their points on items like snacks and drinks. I had a physical and very visceral reaction to this idea, and I passively refused to even set up an account on this system. It was a direct contradiction of everything I'd been taught to believe by our former principal, a contradiction to everything I thought was central to how we should address behavior. Our first principal given us a book to read called *Punished by Rewards* by Alfie Kohn. You get the gist of it, and it put together much of what

---

100 This was less than a year ago. What the memory does.

my experience had taught me. This positive behavior plan would not only fail, it would be harmful.

I finally did make an account as a peace offering, but I didn't use it. Or at least not with any consistency. When the store opened, I told my students what time to go. They were sent back with the message for me that I had to accompany them. I was incredulous, not having been ordered to accompany students on a walk down the hall since my *middle school* days in Nashville. But my students wanted their treats (they were *always* hungry), so I trailed them back to the store, maintaining my distance from the whole affair in a rather petulant manner. Not long after that the store, the funding of which was kind of mysterious, began to be open on a less consistent basis. At some point, I think, it pretty much stopped opening, and not because no one earned any points.

Several of us still consulted with our original principal, sometimes for advice and other times to vent. She would always remind us to be careful about choosing the hill we wanted to die on. One of the principal's next initiatives would be such a hill for me.

We all soon noticed a new person hanging around. He was, we were told, a coach for our principal. He would also be the one to introduce the concept of "no-nonsense nurturing" at a professional development session, where he made a big point of always calling on the women first until I urged him to stop. He had that evangelical zeal of a lot of professional development workshop leaders/salesmen. He relied on his personal narrative and personal charm and thought that ought to be enough to be persuasive. Then I heard the piece that made me choose this initiative as my hill.

Part of the process would involve teachers wearing an

earpiece and being coached, in real time, by people at the school who'd been trained in this area. Naturally, the TFA hire I mentioned before jumped at the chance to be trained. I, however, would not be putting an earpiece in my ear. Such a requirement, which included the possibility of this TFA person being my coach, would send me out the door. This time I was not passive about it. I told the principal. Though he was shocked at my reaction, we negotiated a form of coaching that would not involve the TFA person and would never involve the earpiece. I'd chosen my hill and hadn't died.

Things piled up. Shortly after school began, but not before the teachers had already used them quite often, the water fountains were shut off. Signs appeared saying they were being tested and cases of water bottles would occasionally be distributed among the students. The more permanent water dispensers would not arrive until our school, along with more than fifty others, was announced to have failed that testing. In short, there was lead in the water.

In my career, I've attended good professional development, bad professional development, and what seems like irrelevant professional development. I try to take the approach that I can learn at least something from every opportunity, chosen or required. Prior to my twenty-fourth year, I'd never really known anyone who seemed to have so little clue as to how to use professional development time. Agendas for official professional development days were often shorter than haikus and featured hours supposedly devoted to abstract ideas like '"Building Community" or "Data Review." Without any framework for the former, these slots deteriorated into what the journals call "bitch sessions." Without any real knowledge about the latter, such data dives often resulted in having statistics read to us, with little attempt to understand them and seemingly little ability to interpret them.

Maybe it wasn't all bad. We had a lecture hall now. Though the hall somewhat astonishingly lacked air conditioning, it definitely felt more like a collegiate setting. I began to host social justice sessions in the space. One of my colleagues opened a women's center in an unused classroom to help the female students. Though she met with a surprising amount of resistance from our principal, I thought it was a force for good. These small victories, though, couldn't overcome the catalog of awful that was coming our way.

***

We had a student whose attendance was erratic and his work output was minimal. I can't recall the details of it, but I assigned something that caught his eye. He started doing research about perceptions of neighborhoods, including his own, and asked me for some materials for his final presentation. I texted our original principal with the news of what I was doing and for whom. It required no explanation. We were all thrilled. Two days later, the text messages started coming in around midnight. The student was dead, shot and killed right in front of his house.

We all struggled to react, both in terms of how to help students and how to help ourselves. In one of her frequent displays of having her actions match her words, our original principal, having consulted with our new one, stood in the cafeteria both lunch periods and offered hugs to all. It was a rare display of openness on behalf of our new principal and proof of what our founding principal used to remind us— when we make decisions based on what we think is good for students, we generally make good decisions.

He would be the first of four of our students—past and present—to be shot and killed that year. When the second student was killed, someone who'd started his life at our school as an advisee of mine, our new principal wanted to have no reaction. This second student, he argued, was no longer on our rolls and therefore not our concern. As a veteran of being tone deaf, I knew tone deafness when I saw it and winced with pain at this reaction. He would eventually relent.

It would be too disheartening to recount every specific incident that year, but a few are important to highlight. And they were not all deaths. One Friday, researchers from a local university came in to survey the students about their living and educational conditions. When students asked the researchers why they were doing the surveys about questions like student drug use, they explained they used the research to decide what to study, prepare papers and presentations on, and then propose solutions. About six hours later, two of the students who took the survey in my room that morning would be writhing on the ground in the driveway to a nearby strip mall having been injured in a shooting. I wrote a blog post about the incident that captures my feelings in the moment:

I do not carry a walkie-talkie, but I know our administrators carry them to communicate with each other and with security. And I know, or think I know, that the walkie-talkies that the security guards use are district wide. Maybe they are all district wide. Generally, if there's a problem at another school, you can hear it over the walkie-talkies.

Yet when I heard "shots fired" this afternoon, I knew. I knew it was us. I joined the crew of teachers running toward the incident. I am proud to say that I work with a number of colleagues who run towards incidents and not away from them. Two of them, including one who is in the Army Reserves, had first- aid equipment.

It was right after school. I worked on getting students who were milling about back in the building. I tried to walk slowly. I know, during difficult times, that students watch adults, and if adults are troubled, it makes students nervous.

A freshman passed us on his way back into the school and confirmed what I suspected. The "shots fired" had been aimed at our students, and they had been hit. My latest understanding is that one may go home tonight, but the other may need surgery, but should be *OK*.

I didn't know what to do. I looked around. A friend of one of the two was crying, careening around as others tried to hold him back. As his friends were loaded into the ambulance, he shouted to them, "Don't worry; it's on!" Others tried to talk to him.

I found another student. Tears. She started talking through her tears. I could barely understand her. She just wanted to tell what she saw. I tried to get her to say something to the police; she wouldn't. I should have known that.

I went back to the building, to my classroom, shut down my computer, collected my things. I don't know what shock feels like, but I did not feel good. The afternoon custodian apologized for bothering me. I apologized to him. I left.

Ta-Nehisi Coates makes many great points in *Between the World and Me.* One of them is that we've got to stop talking about slavery as a concept. Those were individual people. They had things they loved to do and people they loved. They had favorite songs and things they could cook. They had opinions. They had stories.

I think my students get similarly abstracted. They are part of a narrative. They are inner-city (is there such a thing as outer-city?) black kids. While I cannot say their names, I can say that they are individuals. One loves to write and speak his words. He shakes my hand each morning when he comes to school—not one of those fancy shakes that are making their way around social media—just an old-fashioned one. He looks me in the eye. He cares about his mother and told me recently that he'd read more books if he had them around the house when he was bored.

The other has a million-dollar style. He recently turned in a great piece of writing about *Their Eyes Were Watching God.* I told him to tape it to the inside of his locker, so that if ever doubted he could do it, the evidence would be there. When he read some Coates, he gave him the ultimate compliment: "This guy is raw." When he had to dress up for game days, sometimes he wore bow ties. I kept meaning to ask him how to tie one. I will when he returns. If he returns. I mean, he will be OK Physically. But it might not be a good idea for him to return to our building. Who knows? And if he doesn't return, it won't be after coming back to say good-bye. He will just simply not be back. I will only know for sure when his name disappears from our attendance roster. I hope he'll be back. He loves to argue. Guest speakers would learn his name. They would ask me about him. He would engage with them. Challenge them. They would tell him to go to college. Coincidentally, I spent much of the evening in a different emergency room. A friend and neighbor injured herself while cooking. While I waited for her, I texted my colleagues, trying to figure out who was feeling what, and how we were all going to find out our way to Monday. I pursued something small and petty that was bugging me. I tried to comfort and be comforted. I tried to advise.

I don't know what happens Monday. I encouraged our principal to call a morning meeting. I don't know what I'd say or do if I were him. There will be counselors who will do their best. There will be tears. Those I can handle. It's watching the glazed looks become more permanently etched on students' faces that haunts me. This, their faces seem to say, is the world we live in. And you, you white guy, you teacher, you suburban-dweller, you preacher of college and career and the future, you don't know anything about it.

And I am, not for the first time, shaken. What is *The Great Gatsby* to my students? I know in my head and in my heart that it can speak to them—of the tragedy of time, I think. For Gatsby, that he can't turn it back. That for them, that they don't think they have much. Try telling them. Not Monday. Monday, probably poetry.

I have, without ever planning it, become something of an older hand at this teaching thing. Again, I feel watched, and I will be watching. There will be counselors for the students, good-hearted, but largely ignored, I suspect. Who looks after the teachers?

This morning, we had visitors from a local university in. Every two years, they survey students; it's kind of a health survey. The students, including those two who I've written about above, laughed about the names of the drugs (what is Kong Kong?) and compared notes on other questions. Someone read another out loud: How easy would it be for you to get a loaded gun in ten minutes? More muttering, laughing. After all, though they didn't have to put their names on the surveys, I was there. At one point, a student asked what would be done with the results and the university rep explained how it would be used as data, that she studied aspects of the mental health of teens and would be using that information.

See, the thing is that I know studies take time, but such reports help set priorities, and money often follows priorities. I told my students, including the two I've written about above, that their younger siblings or cousins or friends would be more likely to benefit from their responses. But our students don't think about time that way. And maybe they're right.

You see we need help. And we need it now. And I've got to figure out if I can be part of the group that gives it.

Our school's response to this and other tragedies shows exactly how bad things had gotten. One of our sophomores, a small girl who wrote better than she thought she did and had strong interpretive skills as an actress, stepped out of her apartment with her father and watched him get shot and killed. My first thought was how to get her help. I asked when our school psychologists would be in, since we shared them with who knows how many other schools.

"They won't," I was told.

"Why not?" I asked.

"Because they're not on year-round contracts," I was

told.[101] We were a year-round school, and it was summer.

"So who can we get?"

"There's no one."

I admit, and those who know me will scoff at the understatement, that I was once capable of quite a tantrum, both personally and professionally. I'd like to think that I've improved what I know now as my self-regulation skills, but it's probably more a factor of just getting old. But at that news, I went throwback. I went into full-scale tantrum mode. I was going to call everyone. And then, because the universe has a sense of humor, I couldn't get phone service. I went for a walk and found that instead of being amused by my hubris, the universe was actually looking out for me. Instead of calling who I'd intended to call and saying what I intended to say, I called our city councilman[102] and told him what had happened and what we needed. And soon enough, not only did the student have support when she returned to school, but the city had reached out to the family as well.

By then, I'd had enough. My two closest colleagues, my roommates from my first two years, were in an active job search. My principal asked me about my intentions. I told him I planned to stay as long as he wanted me around. In truth, I gave myself spring break to decide.

And after making my lists and checking them twice and calling those whose opinion I respect, I decided to stay. I really did. I told those same two colleagues as a way of making myself publicly accountable for my decision. Then

---

101 I seriously don't know who I was talking to—I went into my grey zone.
102 I'm still in shock. He lost his election last night.

we returned for the week of meetings before our final quarter with the students.

Early on the morning of the second day, I sent a text to one of them: "I changed my mind."

She replied quickly: "I knew you would."

That's the kind of friend she is.

And you know what? It was a relief. I love where I've landed now. It is hard work. I am pushed every day. Our meetings are (gasp!) useful. My colleagues are astonishingly creative, persistent and insightful. It is, once again, the first year of a new school. I hope this is it for me; I really do. I am still haunted by these words, though: The only thing harder than the first year of a new school is the second one. I am confident that we can make it through to the other side this time. I really am. Despite my (apparent?) demeanor, I seem to have an endless supply of hope.

Rant: One of the Good Days

I get such a good feeling of contentment when things just seem to go right. We finished reading the play *Master Harold* recently, and a surprising number of students were surprised to see it out again in class the next day.

"Didn't we finish reading it?" at least a dozen of them asked. I had a two-day discussion planned. I had an approach I had learned at Exeter all laid out. I had my good open-ended questions ready. And it was okay. There was some participation. Sometimes, there were bursts of energy. "Why did Hally spit at

Sam?" was a popular one as we talked power, family dynamics, and race. But like I said, it was **OK**. It was, not coincidentally, a day when my administrator walked through not once, but twice. Her first visit was the official one and the conversation, as she noted, was dominated by just a few voices, and I probably kept it going too long. She came back later in the day with our professor-in-residence from our partner university, and the conversation was livelier.

Even though it went better, I knew I could not sustain things for even part of the day after. There was just not enough momentum. I decided to go small. Rather than asking big open-ended questions, I selected four key lines from the end of the play and asked the students to choose one and brainstorm ideas about it. They'd had to write about a line before, and few had finished the assignment, and fewer still had done it well. So here was another motive. They could have another chance to complete the assignment (we had a whole faculty meeting about late assignments earlier in the week) or revisit their initial effort (which included my feedback) and finish that. The plan was to bring small groups together according to the line they chose and have them share ideas while those on the outside monitored the discussion or worked on their own assignment. And, remarkably (and you who teach know how rare this is), this is what happened.

I had the intervention specialist with me for much of the day, and we seemed to have finally found our groove. I spent most of my time with the small group discussion and then rotated around the outside when I could. During sixth period, often my most difficult one, I allowed students who asked to listen to music as they worked. One student even apologized for putting on his headphones without permission.[103] And they wrote. The intervention specialist, who has both strong skills and magnetism, drew both her students and others to her to work through the assignment. She used examples from current movies. I pressed others to remember that they were writing about a play. And they wrote. "This really isn't that hard," said one talented but easily distracted student, "when you just sit down to do it." A student who rarely seems awake in class made an incredibly insightful comment. The intervention specialist looked at me, and we both felt the same way; it was all worth it.

Students were getting it. I gave the student a high five, and we both encouraged her to write her thoughts down before she forgot them. I checked in with her, and we agreed. We didn't want to interrupt the flow; there would be no small groups during this session.

With five minutes remaining, I previewed what was ahead for us (something I'd long advertised) and students already had ideas about partners and scenes. This is not much of a rant, I guess. It was, as I said, one of the good days.

---

103 What was going on? He's a nice young man, but an apology? I was pleasantly befuddled. Come to think of it, I spent much of my life in that state.

12
Campus International High School, Cleveland, OH

There were a number of exciting elements about the school before I even attended my first meeting. I was energized by conversations with our principal. We would have a formal relationship with Cleveland State University, which came with a professor-in-residence whose expertise was literacy. We would be building off the base of a K-8 school (Campus International School) that has a solid reputation. We had parents who showed up for events. And finally, we would not only be offering the International Baccalaureate program, we would, unlike in my two previous experiences with it, be requiring it for everyone. There would be "IB for all!" It became one of our rallying cries.

Once I met everyone, I was even more optimistic. If you've made it this far in the book, you have every right to be thinking, "Here we go again!" My colleagues seemed to be a serious, diverse, and passionate bunch. Our first meetings were worthwhile. I know that may not seem like much, but the consistency of how productive we were just thrilled me. I learned about how we were going to incorporate Youth Participatory Action Research. There was only one immediate downside. We'd be starting in a temporary space, one that used to house part of the K-8 school. But we were assured it would only be temporary, maybe even just one semester, and that semester prediction turned out to be true.

Based on my two experiences with it, I love the energy and excitement of starting a new school, of getting to know students and colleagues, of figuring things out. While I was not happy to be floating, the simple fact that our principal was aware enough to schedule classes in such a way that we'd never have to move from one room to another during a passing period was such a welcome delight. Our principal was great about reminding us not to believe the hype that all of our students were going to be geniuses. He told us that we'd have students ready to read at the college level sitting next to students reading on the third grade reading level. Since he knew that, he actually provided us with professional development that matched our needs, and not just in one session, but throughout the year. "Differentiation" can be a buzzword; it can also be a genuine practice. I'm not saying that any of us were brilliant at it, only that we had the support and training to try. Those of you who are not in education probably don't get how amazing that is.

There were some definite highlights during our first year. A trip to Michigan where there was (deliberately) no running water. A lot of exciting work around the novel, *The Hate U Give*. An opportunity to put our motto, "The City is Our Campus" into action by taking any number of easy field trips, including one to a nearby theatre to see *Macbeth*.

In the spring of our first year at JFK 2.0, our principal introduced the mantra, "The only thing harder than the first year of a new school is the second year." And it proved true then, and it's proving true now. But here, thanks to more support in terms of hiring as well as continued support from parents and Cleveland State, we've been more equipped to deal with the inevitable body blows. Also, while our students aren't always angels, there is significantly less (apparent) violence in their lives.

So is this the last, well, chapter? I recently got the "How much longer do you want to teach?" question and that forced me to do some overdue thinking. My principal was wondering about the prospect of me transitioning into more of a hybrid position. While I could only give him a range in terms of number of years, I said a definite "no" to the prospect of a hybrid position. I'm a teacher. After twenty-five years, I'm still standing. And I plan to do it for at least ten or fifteen more.

Appendix1: Teacher Recommendations

If you've stuck around this long, one of three things must be true:

1. You're related to me.
2. You think I might have some worthwhile things to say.
3. Like me, you can't not finish books.[104]

After all of these years of teaching, what have I learned? I want to end this book with recommendations I would make to a fresh-faced, idealistic young teacher just starting out, like I was twenty-five years ago. Use these suggestions to create your lesson plan book (which you should definitely make, at least for the first few years).

Before the Students Arrive

Expect to spend your own money. Depending on where you teach, it could be a lot. So get a frequent buyer card at whatever school supply place is near you, and do your first big trip during the week near the end of summer. Don't wait until the last week; the place will be mobbed. And whatever you do, **buy the good stapler**. Tissues, too. They are both worthwhile investments.

---

104 Seriously, there must be a name for this condition. I can't put books down. The last book I put down was *Infinite Jest*. I was 235 pages into it and was reading it in the dentist's waiting room. When the dentist saw me carrying it in, he asked me what it was about. When I couldn't answer him, I realized that it was time to stop. Still, I had to hide it until it was time for one of my semi-regular efforts to trade-in books. I knew if I saw it, I would feel guilty and keep trying.

Depending, again, on your school, you may want to **buy pencils for your students**. Some people are against this. Students, they say, should be able to manage bringing a pencil to class. They are right, but for some students just getting to school is enough of a challenge. Besides, if they don't have anything to write with, they won't do any work. And don't give me that "If they are not prepared, they will fail, and that'll teach them to be prepared." No, it won't. By the time you figure that out, you'll have wasted a whole quarter. If you have the energy to maintain some kind of trade for the pencils (a school ID, for example), more power to you. I require a "deposit" of some kind in order to borrow an extra copy of a book, but not a pencil. If I have one, a student can have it.

There is some urban design cliche that suggests that instead of making paths at first, planners should wait and see where people walk. **Arrange your room to set yourself up for success**. Where does the trash can go? The pencil sharpener? Where are you going to have students turn in work? Where does your desk go? (And the answer is not the front and center of the room. Consider avoiding the front of the room all together. Consider doing away with the teacher desk. Consider everything.) Classroom design matters. Take your time with it. And whatever you do, **do not set up the desks in rows**. That's about control. Students get the message as soon as they enter. It's a military or prison formation. Some teachers like islands, but I don't like students to have their backs to me. I am a fan of the U-shape. I do wish there could be a button that would allow you to reset the room according to the needs of the day. Setting 1: Discussion. Setting 2: Small Group Work. And so on. Until that's invented, you have to do it. Better yet, teach your students how to do it.

Find out what you can about your students before they come into the classroom. Talk with previous teachers. Read their files. Don't tell yourself or let anyone tell you that you "want to form your own impressions." That's code for "lazy." Look at what you learn as information. You'll still be able to form your own impressions, and if you're a professional, you'll be able to distinguish those opinions from what you find in the file. Do this.

Buy the good shoes. You may not win style points, but you will be on your feet. A lot. This is one of the many steps you need to take to take care of yourself.

The meetings before the start of the year will drive you crazy. If you expect that, anything more will be a bonus. Until we can shake this tradition, they will exist. **Try to get what you can from the meetings that take place prior to the school year,** and don't get yourself worked up about the rest. There will be new initiatives. Be patient. See what is actually going to happen.

Join a professional organization. It's part of your job to keep up on what's going on in your field. Sometimes, schools will support such memberships and conference attendance for new teachers. Ask. Take advantage of this.

I hate Sunshine Clubs. If something happens in my life, I don't want a card and flowers out of some sense of obligation. You may learn to hate them too. **Contribute to the Sunshine Club anyway.**

For all of my reservations, I've always decided to **join the union or association.** There are benefits that can help you on a daily basis and ones that can help you in case of emergency.

If you're a new teacher, you probably don't have a lot of funds set aside for that emergency. Join.

I realize that a lot of things I've recommended involve spending money. Now I'm going to tell you to spend some more. Get advice and **invest**, even if it's a small amount. There are all sorts of charts available to show you that investing a little bit early is better than a lot ten years later. A lot of people who come to your school will seem like slimy salesman. Do your own research. Invest.

Find a mentor. One may be assigned to you, and if that works, great. If not, then listen. Who makes sense to you? It doesn't have to be someone in your own department. It doesn't have to be someone older or more experienced. Find someone who will help you navigate the culture of the school. Someone who will listen.

Join the gym or team or yoga studio or whatever it is you like to do. If you don't build in the work/life balance from the beginning, it will be very hard to add it as you go. And don't treat taking care of yourself as a luxury to be attended to if you have time. The school year is a marathon. Pace yourself.

Find and meet the people with unofficial power. The custodian. The librarian. The person in charge of technology. The school secretary. The counselors. You don't want your first meeting with them to be when you need help pretty quickly or when you are tense because some problem has arisen. Know their names; make sure they know yours.

Get clear on how you are being evaluated. Ask your department chair, your mentor, your union rep, whomever. There's nothing worse than being scheduled for your first conference and being told to bring, for example, the parent contact log you were supposed to keep from the beginning of the year. More on this below.

Figure out how everything works. If you have technology in your classroom, make sure you know how it all works. Is there a remote? Do you have the cords you need? What is the number for the phone in your room? How do you call the office? How do you call security? If there are computer labs or laptop carts, make a forecast and sign up for a few days in advance. I guarantee you won't be the first. School hasn't even started yet, and some of your colleagues already know what they are doing in March. You can always take your name off of the list. Is there an online grading program? Do you know how it works?

The teacher dreams are normal. You are yelling and no one will listen. You can't find your classroom, and you are running out of time. You are suddenly expected to teach honors Chinese. You will have these dreams. Every year. Don't worry about them. In fact, if there comes a year when you don't have them, then you should worry.

Count your books. Make sure you have enough for everyone on your roster and the inevitable two or three more who will get added to your roster. Don't forget yourself. (In my brief flirtations with administration, I found the last minute requests for a few more copies to be especially annoying. Count ahead of time.)

Find good lunch company. If you're an introvert, make a commitment to eat lunch with others at least once a week. No matter what you are, don't hang around toxic people who complain a lot. It will wear on you and may even become contagious. Try not to talk about school during lunch.

Plan something to do the night before your first day. Your mind will be racing in a zillion directions. You'll check and re-check your bag, your outfit, whatever. Find a silly distracting movie to watch. Something. Make sure you sleep.

Dress well. Odds are, there can't be any requirements about how you dress. Ask your mentor. Watch how people you grow to respect show up at school. Do that. When in doubt, go higher. I tend to wear a shirt and tie. If there are casual days, don't go overboard. Coaches can wear athletic clothes; art teachers can wear messy ones. Unless you are one of those, dress nicely.

Write a syllabus. This will likely be a requirement. I don't agree with it. Students file it and rarely consult it. Parents pick it up at open house and only consult it if they want to argue with you about something, especially grades. Don't sweat it. You're going to make a mistake. Or leave something out. It doesn't matter.

Figure out the grading policy. If the school has one, follow it. If your department has one, follow it. If you are allowed to make your own, make it easy for yourself. You are about to start receiving a blizzard of paper or documents or whatever (we hope); figure out your system for collecting it, organizing it, entering it into the gradebook, and returning it. Figure out your system for late work. What's the school policy for excused absences? Unexcused absences? Suspensions? Extra credit is a debatable beast, but figure out your thoughts on that as well.

Overplan and expect not to get to all of it. You don't want to run out of things to do during the first week or so. That said, there will be constant interruptions, schedule changes, assemblies, fourth period will get behind second period, etc. Figure out what's essential and build from there.

Figure out shortcuts. If you are supposed to have objectives on the board, can you pre-print something like, "After this class, students will know and be able to do"? What can you do to save yourself time? Where will you keep the inevitable cascade of paperwork? Do you know what you need to keep to renew your license? Where are you going to keep it? Trust me, you don't want to have to scramble to find or replace it in three or five years.

If possible, **decorate your room**. Bright, colorful. These are good things. I'm lousy at bulletin boards, but you will soon find students who love to make them. Don't overdo it. Students, especially some students with special needs, can find such things overwhelming.

Set up your teaching journal. I'm still partial to notebooks. You may want to do yours online. Commit to writing in it on a regular basis. It's a place to put reminders so you make different mistakes next year. It's a place to write those emails you shouldn't send. It's a place to doodle during faculty meetings. It's a place for your "to do " list. Keep a journal. You'll thank me when it's your turn to write your book.

Read IEPs. Ask questions if you don't understand them. Get to know the learning and intervention specialists. Figure out how you can best work together. You need these folks.

If you are sharing a room, **have the roommate talk**. How are you going to divide up the space? What are your pet peeves? What are your roommate's? Can you be in the classroom when he or she is teaching? (If not, where can you work?)[105]

Teachers can be stupid about **desk chairs**. Don't be one of them.[106]

The School Year

I presume that you know that cliche about **"Don't smile until Thanksgiving"** is garbage. If you didn't, now you do.

Someone will probably tell you to greet students at the door. If you can, at least the first day, great. I've always found it difficult to be consistent about it, so I don't. **Learn names and learn how to pronounce them correctly.** If someone wants to be called by a middle name or a nickname you are comfortable with, make a note. Memorize names as fast as you can. Make a game of it so they know you are trying. I often use a seating chart and tell the students that their seats will no longer be required once I learn names, but I reserve the right to re-institute it on a case-by-case basis if students demonstrate that they can't make good choices.

This one might be hard, but I'd suggest that you **do not do syllabus stuff the first day**. They've probably already had the syllabus talk four times and expect to have it a few

---

105 I once had a roommate who had a loose relationship with the clock. In short, she was always late, left the room a mess, etc. Finally, I stopped covering and would leave the room so her students would be unattended. I started documenting her lateness, how she left the room, etc. I submitted it to the principal, who thanked me. And he made a programmatic change, and we no longer offered the courses she taught. She was back soon enough as a sub, though. Still, it was progress.

106 I once inherited a classroom from a teacher who retired. When I went into the room the first time, I was impressed with the desk, the chair, the bookcases, the filing cabinets, etc.. When I returned the next day, much of it was gone. I did not, I was told, deserve it.

more. You will sound like a teacher in a Charlie Brown special if you become part of this parade. If you must do something with it, just hit the highlights. Then move on to something useful (a writing sample) or (gasp!) fun. Recently, I've asked students to, in writing, tell me their stories. I still get letters that are pretty bland, but when a student gets into it, it's a beautiful thing.

Take the time to **get to know your students; let them get to know you**. I always have trouble with this one. I am ready to dive into all of the content. Or perhaps I feel pressured to get to all of the content. But taking your time at the beginning will pay off in the end. You will have to **make a decision about privacy** because students will ask you just about everything. I've been asked about my religion, my health, my kids, my salary—just about everything. This goes for **social media** as well. I've got colleagues who set up separate teacher accounts for these things. That's too many passwords for me. You can "friend" or "follow" me after you graduate.

Staff lunchrooms can be strangely toxic places, full of complaints, gossip, and negativity. Most of the time, I avoid them. Periodically, someone (see, perhaps, the Sunshine Committee) gets the bright idea to have a staff potluck. These you should attend. After these lunches, compliments will be exchanged and recipes asked for. Whatever else was true about the recipes, they invariably ended with ". . . and two sticks of butter."[107] Make yourself a goal. Eat in the lunchroom once a week.

I know it's incredibly time consuming, but make those **introductory/positive calls/emails** as soon as you can. If you

---

107 Another time, I will tell you about strawberry pizza.

can't get to everyone, start with your advisory and then move to the students who quickly demonstrate that they will have a big role in your classroom. Let the word spread that you make phone calls. And that first phone call will definitely make that second one easier, regardless of the message. At the American School in London, I made a commitment that for each call or note of concern, I would make a positive contact as well. It was a challenging, but worthwhile plan.

Find a starting point. I usually ask for a writing sample, something expository, something (I hope) that bears no relation to the "what I did on my summer vacation" essay. I might also ask for an argument piece, something students can write without doing any research. I know what their skill level is supposed to be; I want to find out what it really is. If you're in a good department, you'll all do something diagnostic and compare notes. Don't concern yourself with where you're supposed to start the year; start the year based on what you find out from your diagnostic assessments.

Slow and steady wins the race. Keep up with your grading. If you have two different preps (and I hope you don't have more[108]), try to stagger your due dates, so you're not getting hit with papers from every student all at once. I generally grade things in a timely manner, but struggle to return them after that. Returning work never feels like the most important thing I have to do that day. If it's a draft of something the students need to continue working on, that's

---

108 If you do and / or if you are assigned to more than two classrooms, it is probably time to find your Union Representative and make sure what's happening is okay. We continue to do the stupid thing of hazing new teachers to make their lives even more challenging than they already are.

one thing. But if it's a one-and-done assignment, it may gather some dust with me. I have to work on that.

You're human. You will have bad days. Life will be distracting. You'll overreact to a student's behavior. You'll send an email you wish you could have back. Forgive yourself. You get to return the next day. Nobody, I mean nobody, bats a thousand. I worry about those who claim they do (because this means they blame any problems on the students).

Don't think of one class as "the bad class." It'll become a self-fulfilling prophecy. It's called confirmation bias. If you expect them to be the bad class, then that's what they'll become.

You're all on the same side. Everyone (parents, administrators, teachers, custodians, etc.) wants the same thing—for the students to succeed. Try to avoid falling into the "us and them" or, more accurately, the "us vs. them dichotomy." It's awful. When I was in middle school (I think), I spent a day as the secretary's assistant. I was terrible at it. I must have disconnected or mis-transferred dozens of callers, and they mostly didn't care that I was a student. I've always thought that the same thing should happen with students and cafeteria workers, as well as teachers and administrators. I once traded places with the first grade teacher as an April Fool's joke. I only made it for half a day. My point? We all have hard jobs; we (should all) want the same thing.

If you still haven't figured out how **the evaluation process** *really* works, do that. Get some help. You are likely not the only one who is going through it for the first time. Your mentor can help here. The process, the jargon—all of these things will feel ridiculous. Think of the process as checking boxes. I'm not saying you shouldn't concern yourself with it; I *am* suggesting that you keep it in perspective. Staying up all night to craft the perfect lesson plan won't help. Your observer *will* find something to critique. You'll almost certainly disagree or think it's a very small thing. Remember, someone is supervising your supervisor. Your supervisor *has* to have something to say.

I've endured roughly nine million staff conversations about **cell phones**. Do I think they are problem? Yes. While I appreciate the various educational apps and the quick access the students have to a computer in their pocket, all of the policies and apps and rules in the world are not going to stuff this particular genie back in the bottle. We were just asked to draft a cell phone policy, so that we could try to be consistent.

If I spent all of my time chasing illicit cell phone users, I'd lose my mind. It's so easy for this to become a mixed message. On the one hand, we are told, these are the students these days—plugged in and tuned out. On the other hand, cell phones are the scourge of the educational universe, and we must be ever vigilant against their intrusion into the classroom. I don't know of any way to "win" this one. I generally go with a "damage control" approach.

I do get a bit **obsessive about other details**, though. When you walk in, you get your materials out first; you don't wait until you are asked. And this means not just having a pencil, but a *sharpened* pencil. Being on time means being ready to start when the bell rings, *not* just getting into the room. To the best of your ability, set up procedures for whatever you can anticipate. How and where does homework[109] get submitted? What if it's late? Where do students pick up handouts? Where do they pick up yesterday's handout? Where should they put handouts?[110] Where do they find the homework assignment? Where is the bell work or "do now" or whatever it's called where you work? If you are storing items for them, like writing folders, how can you arrange them so that there is not a crowd trying to pick them up all at the same time?[111] If you have a classroom library—and you should[112]—when and how can students check out books? If there is a class set of textbooks, how is that going to work? What about laptops? **All of these things have to be taught.**

Just when you've had a chance to breathe, you will be reminded about **Parent Night or Open House or Back to School Night.** It's probably a Thursday night. Find out what's expected and then find your mentor and ask what

---

109 Then again, should you be giving homework?

110 I was fortunate enough to observe a teacher in Minnesota who maintained an ideal notebook in the front of the room. Students were invited to check theirs against the ideal one to make sure they were staying organized. Another great suggestion I got came from a colleague at the same school. He said I should call up students one at a time and set a timer. Then I should ask for three items they have been told to save—perhaps the syllabus, the instructions for an upcoming assignment, and the reading calendar for a current book. If they can't find all three within a minute, they aren't organized. It was brilliant. And fun. I've never managed the ideal notebook piece. I'm not that organized. But if you've ever looked into the abyss that is a teen-ager's backpack, you know they need help.

111 Try alphabetically rather than by period. If you have them by period, then when period six goes to collect them, you'll have a traffic jam. I have another colleague in Minnesota to thank for this.

112 And here's the key—you should, *no matter what subject you teach!*

she or he does. Have certain basic information on your boards. Have handouts ready. You will be reminded and your administration should remind parents that this is not a night for conversations about individual students. Stay strong. Be ready to make appointments. Have your phone number and email posted. Do not discuss how an individual student is doing. You will be exhausted the next day; make a plan that's easy on you.

Get involved. A school, depending on its size and ambition, has a million extra needs. Some come with a stipend;[113] others don't. Better that you choose something that you like or can at least tolerate, before you get assigned something, like the cafeteria committee[114] or the development committee.[115]

Figure out how the sub system works. You don't want to be caught unprepared if something comes up. And if it's your first year, or your first year in a new building, you will likely get sick. I had bronchitis and walking pneumonia in Nashville. Don't be as stubborn as me. If a day off now will save you two weeks of misery, take it. The sun will come up without you being in school. Do your best to idiot-proof your plans. Some districts have very low standards for substitutes. A good sub is gold. She or he might even help the students accomplish something in your absence. Get the person's name, sub number, phone number, email, and favorite kind

---

113 As we speak, I am earning an astounding $374 for being the chess team advisor.

114 American School in London

115 The Harvard School—and this experience deserves its own made-for-TV movie

of chocolate. Protect that information like you would that of a good babysitter. If you get somewhat remotely competent, try to use that person consistently until you find someone better. Familiarity is helpful. Some subs even learn students' names. And if the sub says someone misbehaves or the sub made an adjustment to an assignment, you have to roll with it.

Progress reports are usually due in mid-semester. There is a certain breed of students who lies in wait for the announcement of such days. Though you are careful to keep your deadline a secret, they find out anyway. And, if you are not prepared, they will present you with a thick stack of work, the density of which would qualify it as a deadly weapon. Do not allow this. Post your deadline. Then post your deadline for pre-progress report work *and your limit*— as in, "You may turn in up to three missing assignments by Thursday, October 6, and they will be graded in time for progress reports." Seriously, I don't know where or when this breed of students originated, but if you encourage them the first time, they will just multiply. As for the progress reports themselves, you will probably get guidelines. Sometimes, you will just have to fill in codes and the computer will spit out your chosen comments. You'll likely notice that there are always more negative choices than positive ones. If there are a zillion to choose from, make yourself a short list of your favorites. If you're told that progress reports are optional for students earning a certain grade or above, don't take the bait. I mean, you do want to make sure that parents are aware of things, especially the possibility of failing, but we don't want to contribute to the idea that communication between school and home only happens when something is wrong.

If you get to (and though it's time consuming, it is also a sign that you're at a good school) write narrative comments, make them specific. Don't just write a fill-in-the-blank template that explains what you've been doing in class and what that students' grades have been for each assignment. That's insulting. Show that you know the student and have something concrete and useful to say. And if there's no process in place for your comments to be proofread, then do it yourself or ask someone you trust.

Parent conferences can be dicey. I started my career by putting out three chairs, but soon realized that involved a potentially awkward assumption, namely that two parents and one child would be attending. The empty chair(s) always seemed like a criticism. So I put out one, and there are others readily available.

Sometimes, parents want grades and test scores, so you should have them ready. But try to make it about more than that. What can you learn about your students? Some parents will come ready to argue. If a conversation becomes uncomfortable, end it. Make an appointment for the future and have someone else (your department head, an administrator you trust) there. I don't like the ten-minute cap. And the process of signing up online has made the whole thing seem like buying concert tickets. It's treating parents like cattle, much the way we treat the students as we shuttle them from room to room based on the bell. Take notes on the conferences. Who has agreed to do what? And don't let parents dump it all on you. "Call me every Friday." "Fill out this form every week." "Email me as soon as there is a behavior problem." Nope. Do none of these. You have a phone number. Parents can call you. Odds are, there is online access to your gradebook. The parent can check for missing work. That is, if parents show up.

At JFK in Cleveland, we'd often have these seven-hour marathon sessions. Parents could show up whenever they wished. And for the most part, they didn't. If we got seven families in seven hours, I was thrilled. And of course, two were always the proverbial "parents we didn't need to see." What was frustrating is that we did nothing original or creative about it. We continued to do the same things we'd always done and continued to be surprised by the results. If parents didn't come to us, should we go to them? Should we have the conferences at a community center rather than the school? Some parents have bad memories of their own school experiences and hesitate to enter such places. Would it help if we offered babysitting? Vision checks? Tax help? Food? Would requiring appointments make it seem more valuable to families? If family contact with schools is important, and in general I think most people agree that it is, we need to be prepared to be more creative.

These conferences can sometimes get intense. You will hear parents talk with their children in ways you probably don't like. You may find yourself in the middle of some long-running tension that's about much, much more than just your class. Try not to judge. Try to keep the conversation focused. These are the kinds of times when I am grateful for time limits.

Learn how to work with a translator. Maybe you knew this, but I didn't know you are supposed to look at the person you are speaking to rather than the translator, and even when the translator is relaying comments back to you, you are still supposed to look at the person who said them initially. Instead of training me on this practice, St. Paul schools let me flounder. I'm sure I insulted many before it was explained to me. Even then, it was hard to adjust. We are used to looking at the person who is speaking to us.

When it's time for **end of semester grades** (if your school is on semesters, if you have grades), beware of grade-grubbing students (and parents). Set a deadline for overdue work and a limit to how much work you'll accept. These grades *count*, so if there's a borderline, go up.

January to March has always been the most difficult time of the school year for me, probably because I've tended to live in cold weather cities. There's not much sun. Even if there isn't much snow, once it hits, it stays and turns grey. Everyone is sniffling. The Sunshine Committee will try to do something. This is when you need to make that gym membership worthwhile. Keep in mind that **April and May**—if you're at a public school—will be consumed by testing. This is really your last chance to do anything sustained. Also, you will be subjected to a great deal of professional development during the year. Try to find something you want to do. Sometimes, schools even have funds to support first year teachers who want to pursue such opportunities.

There's only so much you can really do to help your students get ready for **standardized testing**. Students need to be familiar with the format of the test, especially if it's online. They need to know how to "read" the test and understand what it is they're being asked to do. If you can, and this can start at the beginning of the year, design your assessments so they resemble these tests. Have your students practice their word processing skills. Not only is teaching to the test a bad idea, it doesn't even work.

As the school year winds down, the conversation will probably turn toward **contract renewal** for the next year. Unless there's a compelling reason to leave, you should try to stay. One year at a job on a resume will generally prompt a question. Still, it doesn't hurt to pay attention to the process and the timelines in case you do opt to make a move after two years.

Make a plan for the summer. What are you going to do? Where are you going to go? Unless your finances dictate it, I'd avoid teaching summer school. Do something that will recharge your batteries, not drain them more.

The end of the year will be on you before you know it. There will be performances, concerts, field trips galore. There will be a renewed struggle from students (and parents) to avoid failing. Make sure you know the rules and the timeline. Communicate. No one should be surprised to find out they've failed. I'd avoid offering extra credit (especially for those who haven't done their regular assignments). You should get a checklist about what you need to do to close up shop. If one doesn't seem to be forthcoming, ask for it. There can be a lot of anguish about bulletin boards, for example.

Write in your journal one last time. You will end the year with all sorts of ideas about what you want to do differently next year. I'm not saying they are all good ideas, but you shouldn't lose track of them. Then put the journal someplace where you'll find it in a few months.

And exhale.

Appendix 2: Glossary of Common Terms Used in Meetings and Professional Development Sessions

---

10,000-foot view—The bigger picture (Blake).

A bigger conversation—Translation: "I am not getting the response I want, so I'm going to push for us to put this item back on the agenda, so I can win the war of attrition and get what I want" (American School in London, Blake).

Accountability—How do we hold students accountable for what we taught them? How are we held responsible for how our students do (grades, test scores—mostly the latter)? Translation: Who is to blame (Everywhere)?

Advisory—See homeroom. Place for attendance, paperwork, and really, nothing else (Everywhere).

Diversity—Your guess is as good as mine.

Grit—Small, loose particles of stone or sand; it has no other meaning.

Growth mindset—"I think I can, I think I can, I think. . ."

Low-hanging fruit—A goal that speakers who obviously

never studied Greek mythology thought would be easy to accomplish (Blake).

Multiple intelligences—"Full of sound and fury, signifying nothing."

Perspective—What some teachers say they've taught you if you agree with them (Blake).

PLC—Meeting. It's another name for another meeting (Harding, then elsewhere).

Post-meeting—Name for that time after the meeting when people, especially those without children, linger to discuss things still more because the previous ninety minutes were not enough (Blake).

Privilege—What other people have if they disagree with the speaker (Blake).

Restorative justice—A great concept, honestly. Not so much the decision to commit to it in an inconsistent and sometimes superficial manner (Cleveland).

Rigor—How do make sure the noisy parents don't complain; often confused with assigning more work (Hume-Fogg) rather than challenging work.

SLO—Seriously? Who approved this name (Shaker Heights High School, both schools in Cleveland)?

SMART goal—An oxymoron (first at Harding; eventually, everywhere).

Standards—hat big binder gathering dust in the corner of the bookshelf; see also *Common Core* (everywhere, all the time).

Tone—Undetectable, at least by me (everywhere, all the time).

Transparency—What you show when you are being honest about your thoughts and processes; when I do it, I am revealing state secrets (Blake).

Writing across the curriculum—"Hey, I make my students do words too, you know." (everywhere).

Acknowledgments

Thanks to Dan Crissman, Anne Trubek and everyone else who helped move this from an idea to some blog posts to a book.